AF279943

Patrick Naef

The Technology Illusion

Dispelling the Myth of
Digital Transformation

Contents

Bibliographic information published by the Deutsche Nationalbibliothek
The Deutsche Nationalbibliothek lists this publication in the Deutsche Nationalbibliografie; detailed bibliographical data is available online at https://dnb.dnb.de.

The Technology Illusion: Dispelling the myth of digital transformation

© 2025 Patrick Naef

Text: © 2025 Copyright Patrick Naef

Cover: © 2025 Copyright ACENT AG

Responsible for content:
Patrick Naef / ACENT AG
Friedrichstr. 171, D-10117 Berlin

kontakt@acent.de

ISBN: 978-3-8192-0718-1

Printing/Publisher: Verlag: BoD · Books on Demand GmbH, Überseering 33, 22297 Hamburg, bod@bod.de. Printed by: Libri Plureos GmbH, Friedensallee 273, 22763 Hamburg, Germany.

*"The machine does not isolate man
from the great problems of nature
but plunges him more deeply into them."*

ARTHUR C. CLARKE

*"Science and technology revolutionize our lives,
but memory, tradition and myth frame our response."*

ANTOINE DE SAINT-EXUPÉRY

About the author

Patrick Naef is a partner at Acent AG and the founder and CEO of ITvisor GmbH, a boutique consulting firm specialised on advising organisations on their digitalisation journey. He is also a managing partner at Boyden Global Executive Search and a member of the board of directors at the Franke Group, a global industrial company headquartered in Switzerland. He is chairman of the board of directors at UpGreat AG and senior advisor in the Travel & Transportation practice of McKinsey & Co.

He also advises and supports several technology start-ups, serves on advisory boards of venture capital firms, lectures on digital transformation and business models in the digital age at universities in Europe and the United States.

From 2006 to 2018, Patrick Naef was the Chief Information Officer (CIO) of Emirates Airline & Group in Dubai. During this time, he was also a member of the board of directors at SITA, a global telecommunications and IT services company. From 2006 to 2014, he was CEO of Mercator, an Emirates Group subsidiary that provides IT products and services to airlines around the world. In the late 1990s, he was a founding member and CTO of the start-up Beyoo, the first European online travel portal. He previously served as CIO of Swissair and SIG Group and held senior positions at HP.

In 2011, he was recognised with the prestigious CIO of the Decade award by Germany's CIO Magazin and IDG Inc. He holds a master's degree in computer science from the Swiss Federal Institute of Technology Zurich (ETH), Switzerland and an executive MBA from the University of St. Gallen (HSG), Switzerland.

Acknowledgements

This book would not have been possible without the tireless support of many remarkable people to whom I would like to express my most heartfelt gratitude. I would like to thank Robby Wirth and ACENT AG for their invaluable assistance and steadfast commitment, which were crucial to the success of this book. I would also like to thank Dr. Olaf Röper and Claus-Peter Gutt for their unique expertise and timely advice, which greatly enriched the project. Carola Jacobs deserves special recognition for her consistent support and professional coordination of everyone involved in producing this book. Warmest thanks are also due to my beloved wife Marion Marten-Naef, who dealt so patiently with my typos and awkward wording. Sending my daughter Sophie to British schools also paid off when she kindly helped me with proper British spelling and grammar. I would also like to express my sincerest appreciation to Nina Seitz, Ute Hamelmann, and Talia McCune for creating the illustrations and graphics. The English edition of this book was developed in collaboration with Sean Lothrop.

Finally, I would like to thank the numerous colleagues, CIOs, CEOs, university professors, venture capitalists, and industry leaders with whom I have had countless discussions over the years on the subjects presented in this book—a perfect illustration of the potential of swarm intelligence. This work would not have come about without their collective contributions, trust, and encouragement. My sincere gratitude goes out to all of them.

Patrick Naef

Foreword

As part of our ACENT consultancy projects, I have seen many approaches to digital transformation. After initial experiments with digital subsidiaries and digitalisation strategies independent of company strategy, most digital initiatives today have a clear connection to core business. A digital focus is now typically embedded in the corporate strategy, and the duties of CDO and CIO are increasingly being combined into a single role. For much of the business world, the digital reality has arrived.

Nevertheless, companies do not always exploit their full digital potential, and many limit themselves to the digitalisation of business processes. This approach is not wrong, but it is fundamentally no different from what firms have done with information technology for decades. We have simply replaced the word "automation" with "digitalisation" while failing to recognize and leverage the possibilities offered by true digital transformation.

A comprehensive digital transformation requires a new way of thinking. It is not enough to digitalise existing processes. To survive in a highly competitive global marketplace, business models must be continually tested, redesigned, and upgraded to incorporate the latest digital technologies. Firms must design customer-centred solutions comprising physical and digital products, develop data-driven company processes, and integrate external digital services into existing products. For many firms, this is a journey into the unknown, and traditional industries in particular have very few practical, tested examples from which to draw lessons.

This book will serve as a valuable guide for firms seeking to maximize their digital potential. Patrick Naef is an experienced practitioner, who in his many years as CIO in various industries has successfully implemented numerous digitalisation and transformation projects. Much of Naef's career has focused on air travel, an industry that has been transformed by technological innovations, and this to a larger degree than most other industries. Just a few years ago, many of the digital services that we now routinely use during air travel were conceivable only to a handful of technological visionaries.

Naef's work demonstrates its value right at the outset by drawing a clear distinction between "digitalisation" and "digital transformation". The "digitalisation" process, though widely hailed, often entails little more than the adoption of new technologies. "Digital transformation," by contrast, requires the extensive reorganization of business processes and models, and Naef describes the opportunities and associated challenges in detail, using many practical examples. Understanding information technology not as a supportive tool but as a strategic partner in the company is a leitmotif throughout the book.

Naef's four-stage maturity model for corporate digital transformation is especially useful. The "hybrid companies" described in the fourth stage, which employ a combination of traditional and digital business models, illustrate a new dimension of digital transformation. Firms such as Amazon, Uber, and Airbnb have recognised that personal contact with customers and direct control over physical products are not only consistent with a digital business model, they also open up new business possibilities and enable more effective quality assurance.

Building upon the four-stage maturity model, the book provides many practical recommendations for implementing a digital transformation at the corporate level. Naef highlights the importance of ensuring that boards of directors possess adequate technological skills, describes how to create flexible networks, and details the ground-breaking concept of the quantum organisation – a new corporate paradigm for the network age that replaces traditional hierarchical structures.

With this book, Patrick Naef offers a clear and practical guide for managers who recognise the strategic value of information technology and wish to successfully shape the digital transformation of their companies.

Robby Wirth
Board Member, ACENT AG

Introduction

In recent years, digital transformation and digitalisation have become critical issues that all companies must contend with, even those whose core business is not directly related to digital technologies. Unfortunately, surging interest in the subject has resulted in a great deal of nonsense being written on the subject of digital transformation, and a growing number of self-proclaimed experts are hawking questionable strategies to business leaders. Many of those leaders have little meaningful experience with the latest digital technologies and lack a clear understanding of their utility and potential, making them easy targets for anyone who can convincingly lay claim to expertise.

Very few firms can boast of having fully implemented a comprehensive digital transformation, and most attempts to date have been partial or incomplete. Nevertheless, there is no shortage of people who will eagerly announce that they have led successful digital transformations many times over. Anyone who claims to be a specialist in digital transformation with an impeccable track record should be treated with suspicion.

Much of the gulf between perception and reality in this area – the questionable efficacy of "experts", the dubious veracity of "success stories" – stems from the fact that the essential concept of digital transformation is neither clearly defined nor widely understood. Asking ten of these so-called experts to define digital transformation would probably yield eleven different answers, because most of them have no precise idea of what it entails.

I make no claim to possess a single authoritative definition, but I can offer a simple one that makes sense to me. The first step is to distinguish between "digital transformation" and "digitalisation". Although these terms are often used synonymously, they refer to very different processes, goals, and outcomes. Differentiating between the two terms is the first step toward understanding them.

Digitalisation vs. digital transformation

Though the terms "digitalisation" and "digital transformation" are often used synonymously, the two concepts differ in important ways. "Digitalisation" means *using information technology to automate existing processes within established business models and markets*. Implementing an enterprise resource planning (ERP) system to automate financial, human resources, and material management, or using robotic process automation (RPA) or artificial intelligence to assume administrative functions currently performed by workers are examples of the digitalisation of internal corporate processes. Marketing existing products and services available via websites and mobile apps is an example of the digitalisation of sales channels. Automating transactions with external suppliers, distributors, or other partners is an example of the digitalisation of supply chains. Though continually evolving, digitalisation is not new at all. It began when the first computers arrived on the market and started to supplant formerly manual processes.

By contrast, "digital transformation" is *the use of information technology to exploit new business models or markets, to redesign core processes, or to develop wholly new products and services*. Unlike digitalisation, which focuses on increasing the efficiency of existing processes and systems, digital transformation involves fundamentally altering the way in which the firm does business.

Examples of digitalisation and digital transformation:

Digitalisation

Cashpoints (ATMs): A new technology makes performing simple bank transactions more convenient, but the actual process of withdrawing money remain largely unchanged for the customer, and cash is still issued to the customer in the form of physical banknotes.

In 1939, Turkish-born Armenian George Luther Simjian, an inventor of numerous devices and holder of more than 200 patents, developed and assembled the first cashpoint – the so-called "Bankograph". City Bank of New York, now known as Citibank, put the new machine into use, but it was not a success. Gamblers and sex workers were the only customers who dared to use the newfangled devices. The Bankograph failed to gain widespread acceptance and was taken out of service a mere six months after being installed.

In 1965, Scotsman John Shepherd-Barron arrived at his bank just before closing. Although he was able to cash his cheque at the last minute, the experience continued to vex him. Why were there machines that could dispense chocolate bars, but none that could dispense cash? He pondered the problem and eventually came up with an initial design for a cash-dispensing machine. Within two years, Barclays Bank had produced six prototypes of Shepherd-Barron's invention, and the first of the machines was put into operation on 27 June 1967 in Enfield, north of London. The modern cashpoint was finally born.

As the invention was refined, its range of functions steadily expanded. Banks wanted to enable their customers to complete most of their banking transactions at the machine and at any time, day or night. Cashpoints would enable banks to pare back their teller staff while increasing the frequency of customer interactions. Though the advent of cashpoints has permanently altered how banks engage with customers, the machines merely automate services previously performed by human staff. Bank business models remain unchanged.

Moreover, new technologies have begun to supplant the services of cashpoints. With the arrival of digital payment methods such as credit and debit cards, mobile banking, and peer-to-peer payments, cash is gradually becoming less important, and so are cashpoints. These newer systems gained further traction during the COVID-19 pandemic, and in the future they could replace cashpoints entirely. This example illustrates a key feature of digitalisation: it is typically an iterative process in which new technologies render previous systems obsolete, only to be outmoded in turn.

Online check-in for air travel: Electronic check-in kiosks at airports reduce waiting times, but the check-in process itself remains essentially the same.

Alaska Airlines introduced the first self-service check-in kiosks in 1997 on a trial basis. The kiosks were designed to shorten waiting times for passengers by allowing them to print out their boarding passes, choose their seats, and receive their luggage tags without having to queue at a counter. While accelerating check-in improved the use of airport resources, even in this example, the check-in process remained essentially unchanged. A physical plane ticket was still exchanged for a physical boarding pass at the kiosk. Human check-in agents were replaced by machines, and the actual work was transferred from the airline's employees to its customers.

With the widespread use of mobile phones and airline apps, neither a physical plane ticket nor a physical boarding pass is required anymore. Instead, each is displayed in digital form in the app. Fully digitalising the check-in process yields further efficiency gains for customers and airlines, though the transition is constrained by the limited uptake of apps among travellers and by their reluctance to trust a fully digital version of an important document. This example highlights another feature of digitalisation: a mix of caution, scepticism, and the inertia of ingrained habits can slow the implementation of new technologies, even when they offer a clearly superior solution.

Digital transformation

Swiss Post: From traditional postal service provider to national digital leader

For 175 years, Swiss Post has connected individuals and firms across the country and ensured the safe transport of information, goods, and people. In the digital age, the postal service has continually adapted to meet the growing challenges and needs of a digitally networked society. The path to a digital future involves not merely adapting to change, but consciously shaping the integration of firms, government agencies, and the people of Switzerland.

Digital communication can now be broadly divided into three areas: business-to-business (B2B), business-to-customer (B2C), and customer-to-customer (C2C). For the first two segments, Swiss Post provides IT solutions that enable rapid, reliable, and, above all, secure interactions. While formal communication dominates in the B2B segment, and companies such as SAP, Microsoft, and Google play a central role, B2C and C2C communications systems rely on a more informal, often mobile communication infrastructure led by Meta subsidiaries Facebook and WhatsApp.

Rather than merely standing by and observing these developments, Swiss Post has helped shape digital communications as a driving force behind a modern, networked Switzerland. As part of its growth strate-gy in 2021, Swiss Post formed a new division, "Digital Services", with a mandate to advance the country's digital transformation by enabling companies, public authorities, health services, and private individuals to exchange sensitive data securely and efficiently. Digital Services in-vests in digital solutions that are simple and intuitive, with a focus on formal B2C and B2B communications. This approach has enabled Swiss Post to transform itself by developing the capacity to provide new dig-ital products and services to new clients via new digital distribution channels.

Netflix: From shipping DVDs by post to a streaming service that now produces most of its content itself

Netflix was founded by Reed Hastings and Marc Randolph in 1997 as a subscription-based DVD rental service. Hastings and Randolph's original objective was to create an e-commerce platform, like Amazon, but exclusively for films. Customers would sign up for a subscription, choose the films they wanted to rent and then have the DVD delivered to their doorstep within one working day. Users could watch as many films as they wanted as part of their monthly subscription.

In the 1990s, the unlimited online DVD-by-mail model was a ground-breaking innovation. This new approach enabled users to rent films on-line and receive them at home without needing to visit a video rental store. When it was launched, Netflix had only a modest catalogue of films for clients to choose from, and it initially faced an uphill struggle. Two years after its launch, Netflix had attracted just 300,000 subscrib-ers. Meanwhile, the high costs of physically shipping DVDs via the US Postal Service plunged the company into a financial crisis. The situation became so serious that Hastings was forced to offer Netflix's compet-itors, Blockbuster and Amazon, shares of up to 49% in the company, but no deal was reached. Blockbuster was the dominant player in the brick-and-mortar video-rental industry at the time and its more conventional model appeared to be thriving.

At the beginning of the 21st century, however, digital innovation dramatically altered the competitive landscape. High-speed internet became increasingly common, and costs dropped significantly. The video-on-demand market, where Netflix was already an established incumbent, suddenly gained momentum. Originally, Netflix had planned to take an analogue approach to replacing physical DVD rentals by developing a portable device onto which films could be downloaded for later viewing. Although this approach offered high-quality services, it was not very convenient in terms of user experience, and it was shortly discontinued. In 2005, Netflix transitioned to a direct streaming platform, which was operational by 2007. A mere 1,000 movies were available for streaming at launch, but the catalogue increased by an order of magnitude over the subsequent two years. The increasing popularity of video-on-demand catalysed Netflix's growth outside of the United States, and by 2016 it had conquered the global market. At the end of 2017, the company had more than 100 million subscribers and one of the highest market capitalisations in the media and entertainment industry. Enabled by the ongoing expansion of high-speed internet and the user-friendliness and interoperability of Web 2.0, Netflix's digital transformation fundamentally altered the market and created a new, more efficient service model.

The four-stage model of digital transformation

Unfortunately, the term "digital transformation" has become a corporate buzzword and nearly every company that launches a new mobile app or automates its internal processes with an ERP system now boasts of having undergone a digital transformation. Merely shifting a company's systems or applications to the cloud or rolling out Microsoft Teams for home office users has very little to do with a digital transformation. Several years ago, a Chief Information Officer (CIO) of one of the larger US industrial companies told me that he had already completed the digital transformation of his company by moving all of its systems to the cloud and giving out iPads to all employees. Well, to me a digital transformation requires a little more than that.

As its name suggests, a digital transformation must be transformational. It must fundamentally alter a company's business model, its value-creation processes, its sales channels, or the products and services it provides. To help ensure that executives fully understand the nature and implications of digital transformation, I have developed the following four-stage "maturity model." Most of the maturity models developed by consultancy firms, such as Capability Maturity Model Integration (CMMI), Cybersecurity Maturity Model Certification (CMMC), or Information Technology Infrastructure Library (ITIL), consist of five stages. If I worked for one of these large consulting companies, I would have probably also thought up a fifth stage, but as I am not being paid by the hour, I can afford to keep things simple.

Stage 1: Digital cosmetics or "lipstick on a pig"

Sadly, this is the stage that I see most often. Companies digitalise for the sake of digitalisation or for reputational reasons, as these days every firm is expected to present itself as a digital company. In many cases, an innovative technology of some kind is introduced somewhere within the company and then exploited for marketing purposes, but it never becomes embedded in core business processes, let alone integrated into the traditional back-end systems. The example I gave above of a CIO colleague who simply shifted the firm's systems to the cloud and distributed iPads to all employees is typical of Stage 1. The goal was not to add value but to be able to claim that they had migrated to the cloud and adopted sophisticated but familiar end-user devices. Beyond this, nothing had been changed in terms of the firm's business model, its organisational processes, or the products and services it provides.

I encountered another example of an alleged Stage 1 digital transformation a few years ago. On a flight from Dubai to Frankfurt, I read an article about a large US-headquartered hotel chain, which the article announced had completed a digital transformation. It described how a new personalised booking site was developed for customers, together with a corresponding mobile app, and it highlighted the introduction of robots in hotel reception areas to welcome and check in customers. The article also praised the chain's new cloud-based loyalty programme, which would ostensibly enable a high level of personalisation.

As chance would have it, I had booked a room at a Frankfurt hotel belonging to that very chain, and I am also a member of their loyalty programme. I had completed the booking on their website, and my information – payment methods, passport details, preference for a non-smoking room, etc. – was stored in my online profile. When I made

the booking, I had the option of indicating the flight on which I would arrive in Frankfurt. On arrival, however, there was no sign of the personalised service described in the article. After making my way from the terminal building, over a footbridge to the hotel lobby, I joined a lengthy queue in front of the reception counter. I waited in the queue for about 20 minutes. When I reached the counter, I explained to the friendly woman working there that I had already booked a room and showed her my loyalty programme membership card. She then asked me for my booking confirmation, passport, and credit card, and she handed me a form to fill out. I had to enter my residential address, mobile phone number, e-mail address, passport number, and other information that I knew was already stored in their systems. She then typed on her keyboard for a couple of minutes, probably assigning me to a suitable room, handed me a keycard, and wished me a pleasant stay. Imagine my surprise when I found that she had assigned me a smoking room, even though the fact that I am a non-smoker is stored right there in my loyalty programme profile. As one might also imagine, I found it quite annoying to have to go back down to the reception area and join the queue again to request a non-smoking room. Check-out was a similarly traditional process: I went to the counter, spoke with a receptionist, and used my credit card to pay for additional expenses. Where was the digital transformation touted in the article?

Obviously, something went wrong during this alleged digital transformation. Let us consider how my customer experience could have gone, had the hotel chain exploited the full potential of the digitally networked world in which we live. I had booked my room online and entered my flight number. My credit card details were already stored in the hotel's system, along with my mobile number, e-mail address, personal preferences (e.g., a non-smoking room), and other information. Had the hotel chain connected its systems with the airport system, the hotel would have been informed when my flight from Dubai landed in Frankfurt. If integrating with the airport system proved challenging, the chain could have accessed one of the numerous websites, apps, and other publicly available platforms that provide this kind of information almost in real time. A simple algorithm could have allocated me a suitable room the moment I landed, prioritising a non-smoking room if one were available. The hotel could have sent me my room number via an SMS, WhatsApp message, e-mail, or notification on the chain's own mobile app, and the NFC chip on my mobile device could have been used as a room key. My credit card number is already stored in my profile, so I could have been charged automatically at check out. Multiple steps could have been eliminated from the process – saving me time and the hotel labour hours – had the chain made sensible use of the information that was either already available to it or that could have been obtained from other systems. The check-in/check-out process could have been almost entirely automated and made obsolete to me as customer, with staff interactions reserved for special requests and troubleshooting, or deployed strategically to put a human face on the experience while still maximizing efficiency.

Why had this hotel chain not managed to effectively digitalise a process as simple as this? I believe the root of the problem was a simple failure to understand the meaning of a digital transformation and recognise its potential. It is not enough simply to carry out a few isolated high-visibility projects involving robots, AI, a mobile app, or a new website, to maintain the pretence of being "digital". This hotel chain was probably more concerned about the marketing effect of digitalisation than about the added value it could achieve for its customers. Introducing humanoid robots in the reception area to automate the check-in process makes little sense if digital technologies can render that process obsolete.

Much like the robots at the hotel reception performing a service that could be fully digital and automatic, many airlines still use physical check-in kiosks in airports to replace check-in counters and agents.

Originally, the main function of airport check-in was to exchange the flight ticket with a boarding pass. This process dates back to the time when physical plane tickets included a coupon (voucher) for each flight segment purchased. Some older readers may still remember the red carbon copies that could once be found attached to plane tickets. At check-in, these copies were removed from the tickets (which were small booklets at the time) and exchanged for boarding passes. A flight coupon was a value document, much like a cheque, as the travel agency or airline that sold the ticket had already been paid by the customer. Because the party that actually performs the flight service and transports the passenger is often not the same party that sold the ticket, the passenger was obliged to hand over the corresponding flight coupon to the airline at check-in. The airline would later use the coupon to claim its share of the ticket price – via a clearing house – from the party that initially sold the ticket and therefore had collected the money. Even though this process remains largely unchanged today, the physical tickets and flight coupons have long since been digitised. As a result, the check-in process no longer requires the transfer of a physical document and can be performed entirely online.

Although checking in at the airport has never represented any real added value for customers, who generally regard it as a time-consuming nuisance, some elements cannot be fully automated yet. Handing over luggage at the check-in counter, affixing a luggage tag with a barcode indicating both its destination and the traveller to whom it belongs, and providing a corresponding baggage receipt to the traveller is still necessarily a physical process that requires some degree of human interaction. Over the last few decades, increased security measures have further complicated the check-in process, as airlines must now ensure that luggage always travels on the same aircraft as the passenger to whom it belongs and that all passengers have the necessary travel documents with them, such as passport and visas, or that they have any required vaccinations and health tests.

Nevertheless, airlines have realised that much of the process can be completed much more efficiently via the internet or a mobile app and that the physical check-in process is no longer required. Virtualised boarding passes displayed on mobile devices have begun to replace paper boarding passes, and passengers now often print their own luggage tags at home and then simply hand over their luggage at a drop-off point at the airport. Even this physical analogue remnant, the luggage tag, will soon no longer be needed, as innovative start-ups such as BagsID are using AI-powered algorithms to recognise items of luggage by their appearance – a type of biometrics for luggage – which can achieve a higher accuracy than traditional tags and a barcode scanner. In some cases, passengers can also use biometrics to verify their identity, though this element of the process remains limited by technological uptake and the security requirements of airports.

Many of these approaches are not entirely new, as we were already implementing them at Swissair in the 1990s using what was at the time advanced technology – though it would seem rather rudimentary today. Our top customers had a loyalty card equipped with an RFID tag, which was also their frequent flyer card. Instead of check-in kiosks, which barely existed at that time, we set up so-called "fast-track gates" at the entrance to the departure gates, where authorised customers could simply walk through. The RFID sensors incorporated into the fast-track gates recognised the passengers, who were automatically checked in and received an SMS message with their respective gates and seat numbers – all without having to queue at a counter. Although this was 25 years ago, long before the advent of smartphones, we had largely automated the check-in-process, though today we would say we had "digitalised" it.

But let's get back to our example with the hotel chain, and my experience as customer. You can imagine how disappointed I was after this experience, particularly since this hotel chain boasted about a digital transformation but had not even managed to digitalise simple process-es in a sensible way, something that we had already automated at Swis-sair 25 years earlier, to the benefit of our customers. Plenty of things fell by the wayside during the digital transformation of this hotel chain. Or, to use a much more diplomatic expression: "There is still room for improvement".

Stage 2: Digital silos

Most companies that claim to have successfully completed a digital transformation likely fall into the second stage, "digital silos." I use the term "silos" with no disrespect, because it is arguably the most com-mon type of digitalisation, but in my view this approach is not actually transformative, since it remains focused on automation rather than on revolutionising a firm's business model.

Companies at the "digital silos" stage automate their existing tried-and-tested business processes through the consistent use of technologies, but they do so solely within their traditional business model and field. They make no significant adjustments to their working methods, culture, or organisational model and remain rooted in their traditional hierarchi-cal structures. As a result, digitalisation efforts remain largely confined to their respective corporate units (silos), under the responsibility or "own-ership" of the manager responsible for each relevant business area or organisational process. Incentive structures also tend to remain focused on the individual goals of each area of responsibility, so that the respec-tive manager has little interest in advancing digitalisation efforts in other business areas, let alone pursuing company-wide transformation.

Stage 2 digitalisation is therefore concerned with optimising lo-cal systems and business areas and ignores the potential for "global"

Marketing
Operations
Production
Procurement
Finance
Digital
IT

digitalisation extending beyond the boundaries of the organisational silo, even when the benefits for the company or consumer would be enormous. Some companies combine such local digitalisation initiatives with organisational restructuring efforts focused on end-to-end value creation – i.e., the shift to a process-driven organisation. However, if the organisation model remains based on strict hierarchical principles, vertical silos are merely replaced with horizontal silos, which does not actually solve the problem of the silos, since horizontal silos also remain silos in hierarchical structures.

For example, a few years ago a good friend told me that he had just received a new car that he had ordered several months earlier from a well-known German car manufacturer. He explained to me how he had been able to configure the car to his personal specifications on the manufacturer's website, selecting features and extras, the interior setup, the paint colour, the engine configuration, etc. After ordering the vehicle, he had been able to track its status on the website as it was being built, at any time during the production process, from ordering right through to delivery. This carmaker had digitalised their production process to a high degree, which enabled them to share data from their internal systems in real time with their customer, thus creating significant added value for the customer.

He then proudly showed me the digitised user manual on his iPad and explained that he no longer needed to keep a thick, heavy physical manual in the car. As I took a closer look at this digital manual, however, I realised that it was not specific to "his" car but rather a generic manual for all models in the range. As such it contained numerous chapters on features, functions, engines, etc. that did not apply to my friend's bespoke vehicle. This experience made me wonder why this leading automotive manufacturer had not managed to produce a personalised digital manual specifically for my friend's car. The necessary information to create one was readily available, thanks to the digitalised order process and the highly automated production process. It would have been easy to produce a manual that described all the features – and only the features – that were available in my friend's personalised vehicle. But no, the manufacturer had simply supplied a PDF version of the generic manual to replace the printed version and nothing more.

What went wrong here? I think this missed opportunity is a direct consequence of digital silos. The organisational unit responsible for production has digitalised its processes to a high degree and has even become connected and networked with the sales department, which had already been using a digital configurator for years – albeit not so much with the customer in mind but primarily to obtain the configuration data to feed into the production process easily and to lower the cost. However, the company failed to extend digitalisation beyond these organisational silos. The department responsible for creating the manuals probably "lives" in its own organisational silo and is not closely linked to either production or sales organisations – or the process of creating the manuals may even have been outsourced to a third-party company. Managerial performance in this department is probably measured by the marginal cost of each manual produced, not by customer satisfaction or the customer experience with a personalised product. A holistic approach that digitalises the entire value-creation process with the customer always in mind, including any outsourced process steps, would probably have led to an even more satisfied customer showing off his highly personalised digital user manual.

I believe that all the attempts made by traditional companies to imitate truly digital businesses such as Uber, Amazon, Google and the like by automating their processes will not succeed unless the organisational structures, culture, and ways of working are also adapted accordingly. This includes breaking up or at least softening rigid hierarchies.

Stage 3: Digital or network business model

Of course, many major companies have built digital business models (or network business models) from scratch. We all know the stories of Uber, Airbnb, Amazon, Facebook, etc., which emerged and grew rapidly in the digital age. Most of these digital companies have one thing in common: they do not themselves produce or provide an actual product or service but instead act as intermediaries between suppliers and consumers. While retailers have always sold goods produced by others, in the digital age this process can be completed with only a fraction of the physical infrastructure that traditional brick-and-mortar retail requires. Walmart, for example, operates thousands of physical stores in which hundreds of thousands of physical products are sold. Its operations require huge warehouses with complicated logistics and employ over two million staff worldwide. Amazon, by contrast, initially had no physical stores, no warehouses, and no logistics of their own, because it merely operated a website on which it matched buyers and sellers of its original product, books. When a customer bought a book on its website, Amazon ordered the book from the publisher and had it sent directly to the customer. Amazon's business model has changed considerably over the years, as it has expanded its range of products by several orders of magnitude and insourced various process steps originally performed by third-party companies, but it remains a truly digital company. I will return to this example in the section on Stage 4.

For a long time, it was said that Amazon maintains no inventory, Facebook produces no content, Uber owns no cars, and Airbnb owns no real estate. These are purely digital business models that thrive by making clever and efficient use of technology to connect supply with demand, all digitally over the internet. The added value of these marketplaces or networks increases exponentially with the number of participants on both the supplier and consumer sides. In social media networks such as Facebook, Instagram, X (formerly Twitter), TikTok, etc., content producers are also consumers at the same time. Exponential scale effects lead to monopolisation or the establishment of a dominant position by a small group of large networks or marketplaces. Ray Wang describes this process aptly in his book, *"Everybody Wants to Rule the World: Surviving and Thriving in a World of Digital Giants"*[1]. In the digital world, there are few unique selling points, and sheer size is crucial. A family-owned corner shop can survive just fine in the "old economy", even if it sells a very limited range of products at higher prices than a large supermarket, because it serves a small group of consumers who will pay for convenience and physical closeness. On the internet, however, there are no distances, and thus boundaries disappear. As a result, buyers will go where they can find the widest range of products and the best prices.

However, focusing exclusively on lower prices is not a sustainable strategy for a digital business. In a context where prices can be compared instantly across sellers at a negligible cost, size becomes the decisive factor, because firms that sell larger quantities can demand lower prices from producers and therefore offer lower prices to consumers, enabling them to entrench their dominant position. This size advantage means that customers will go to the websites where they find the widest selection. Suppliers, in turn, want to offer their products and services where they can reach the most customers, so they flock to the largest sellers, allowing those sellers to expand the range of goods they offer until something close to a retail monopoly is created. On the internet, a small family-owned corner shop with a modest range of the same products that Amazon offers has no chance unless it finds another unique selling point to differentiate itself from the big players.

---

1   Wang, Ray: *Everybody Wants to Rule the World: Surviving and Thriving in a World of Digital Giants.* HarperCollins Leadership, 2021.

The fact that companies with a digital business model do not produce physical goods, do not display them in physical stores and sales outlets, and do not deliver them to the customer via complex and expensive logistics – all of which can be highly labour-intensive – means that these companies can grow much faster than their brick-and-mortar competitors in the "old economy". In fact, they can grow almost exponentially because they do not depend on physical infrastructure or large numbers of staff.

The digital business model is further strengthened when the product is virtualised (or digitalised) so that it no longer exists physically. Amazon took this step with the Kindle, which replaced physical books with digital ones, offering huge advantages:

- Whereas physical books still need to be printed, digital books can be reproduced as often as desired with production costs approaching zero.
- Whereas physical books still need to be shipped, digital books can be distributed instantly and with delivery and logistics costs also approaching zero. Physical books must be stored and delivered, which incurs costs.
- Whereas physical books can be supplanted by new editions, which require an entirely new purchase and delivery to obtain mostly unchanged content, digital books can be automatically updated by the publisher, allowing them to be continually improved and expanded, and thus upgrade costs also approach zero. The same concept applies to highly digitalised products. For instance, a new Tesla model is often just a software upgrade that can be installed "over the air" on an "old" model. Although these costs tend towards zero for Tesla, the company still manages to charge the customer for such upgrades.

Another example from the travel industry can further illustrate the difference between a traditional business model and a digital model:

Uber, the world's largest taxi company, owns no vehicles. **Facebook**, the world's most popular media owner, creates no content. **Alibaba**, the most valuable retailer, has no inventory. And **Airbnb**, the world's largest accommodation provider, owns no real estate.

Something interesting is happening.

Tom Goodwin

If an airline wants to double its revenue, it must also roughly double the size of its fleet and hence also double the staff it needs to operate these new or larger aircraft. The airline's growth is therefore directly dependent on the number of aircraft (i.e. the production facilities) and the size of its workforce. Of course, it is also possible for an airline to grow qualitatively, not merely quantitatively, by enhancing its services, improving its efficiency, or increasing prices. However, in the highly competitive airline industry, the scope for qualitative growth is very limited, and even gains in service quality or efficiency may require upfront investments in new aeroplanes and trained staff. The airline industry is therefore a very traditional industrialised business model in which growth can be achieved almost exclusively through a slow, expensive process of expanding production facilities (aircraft fleet) and onboarding additional personnel to operate them.

On the other hand, digital companies in the travel industry like Uber, Lyft, Airbnb etc. can grow much more quickly because they do not depend on their own production facilities and personnel. Taking on additional drivers at Uber or more rooms at Airbnb can be done in a matter of seconds, while adding new aircraft to an airline's fleet and hiring and training new staff can take years. Even when an airline can lease additional aircraft and source trained personnel externally, such processes can take months or even years.

Conversely, a purely digital business model may be neither sustainable nor future-proof, because ultimately someone still has to produce the products or services being sold using physical production facilities. The "graveyard" of failed companies is full of such digital companies that rocketed to overnight success and plunged back to earth just as quickly. Many once-celebrated digital pioneers such as Yahoo, Myspace, BlackBerry, Netscape, Pets.com, TiVo, Pebble, AOL, AltaVista, MapQuest, etc., have either disappeared or are now mere shadows of their former selves.

Perhaps the solution lies in combining traditional (industrial) and digital business models? This brings me to the fourth and most advanced stage, digital hybrids.

Stage 4: Digital hybrids

When I first created my model of digital transformation for a 2016 presentation at the prestigious Europa Forum in Lucerne, Switzerland, it had only three stages. In the years that followed, however, I realised that the digital landscape had shifted again. After being widely hailed in the media for their fully digital business models, leading and rapidly growing companies such as Uber, Airbnb, Amazon, Alibaba, and Facebook (Meta) came to realize that physical contact with their customers and direct control over the physical products and production facilities (e.g., vehicles, rooms, etc.) could significantly improve quality control and enhance customer satisfaction. In addition, they also recognised that leveraging their technology expertise and hence integrating digital technologies into these physical production facilities could make them more efficient, easier to manage, and more customer-friendly. The ride-hailing service Uber, for example, was originally based on a pure network business model and had no vehicles of its own. Now, however, Uber is investing heavily in the development of its own autonomous vehicles in partnership with major automotive manufacturers. These investments in new technology will enable Uber to steadily increase service quality while also reducing costs.

Other digital companies have followed a similar trajectory: Airbnb has started to buy properties; Amazon is setting up physical stores and logistics - including its own fleet of cargo planes - while Facebook and Netflix are producing their own content. These companies have now become digital hybrids, as what was once a purely digital business model progressively incorporates elements of a traditional industri-al model, with physical production facilities, warehouses, stores, and other infrastructure, along with the associated staff. However, hybrid-isation can also proceed from the opposite direction, with companies supplementing their traditional business model with a digital one. For years, many market observers have assumed that traditional compa-nies were being replaced by digital competitors, but it is now clear that the fusion of digital and traditional business models offers a more promising – and also more sustainable – approach in the long run.

Numerous successful examples of this category of digital hybrids come from the traditional world. For example, John Deere, the long-estab-lished manufacturer of agricultural and construction machinery, has added digital products and services to its offerings and enhanced its products with digital technologies. For decades, John Deere has adver-tised its high product quality and trustworthiness as a brand, as well as its cutting-edge technology, though this was understood primarily as a matter of mechanical innovation, and the only way for customers to get in touch with Deere was by personal contact through their dealers. Today John Deere leads the way in integrating digital technologies to its machines, including telematics, self-driving controls, and remote monitoring capabilities, as well as artificial intelligence (AI), cloud ser-vices, internet of things (IoT), drones, analytics, SmartGrade systems, and other precision technologies that improve both the technical effi-ciency of the machine itself, as well as the operational efficiency, be it in the field or on the construction site. John Deere's intelligent tractors, loaders, and combine harvesters are not only better machines, but now represent a completely new sector, "precision agricultural technology", in which an expanding range of offerings is marketed to an increasing-ly tech-savvy customer base.

Hilti, a manufacturer of drilling machines and other high-quality construction equipment, has made a significant contribution to the

The world's largest taxi firm, **Uber**, is buying cars. The world's most popular media company, **Facebook**, now commissions content. The world's most valuable retailer is now **Amazon**, and has more than 350 stores. And the world's largest hospitality provider, **Airbnb** increasingly owns real estate. **Things change.**

digitalisation of the construction industry. For more than 75 years, Hilti has worked passionately to create a better future for the construction industry. The company has differentiated itself from the competition by offering high-quality products and a direct-sales team that can be on site with customers on a daily basis. In recent years, Hilti has undergone a digital transformation that has enabled the company to boost their customers' productivity. The sales organisation has shifted to a multi-channel approach, enabling customers to purchase products and services directly on the Hilti website, manage or renew all of their fleet rental contracts with a single click, and request repairs for their equipment online and in real time.

There are numerous other examples: Monsanto with its digital "precision farming" services, Franke with its networked and IoT-enabled coffee machines, Vorwerk with their Thermomix and Cookidoo platform, etc.

This was also the strategy we defined at Emirates in the second half of the 2010s, when we saw how new players, such as Uber and Airbnb, entering the travel market with their digital network business models were able to grow much faster than a traditional airline, because – as described above – we were dependent on the limited growth potential of our physical production facilities, our aircraft fleet, personnel, airports, etc. We responded by developing a new strategy that would supplement our traditional industrialised airline business model with a digital network business model.

Our strategy essentially consisted of three pillars, which aimed to expand and improve our business model through the consistent use of digital technologies. We called the first two pillars "hyper-personalisation" and "autopilot operation". Hyper-personalisation used data-driven customer insights to develop tailored offers to our customers and processes to maximise revenues and profit margins. Autopilot operation focused on using AI to highly automate the organisation's operation, ensuring deviation-free, consistent and cost-efficient service delivery. The third and central pillar was the "virtual marketplace." Recognising that our highly industrialised business model limited our growth, we were determined to complement our traditional airline business model with a network business model that would offer additional travel-related products and services to our customers in a digital marketplace under our strong Emirates brand. Much like other digital businesses, these products and services would be produced and provided by third parties, with the Emirates digital marketplace allowing for a high degree of personalisation and automation. Emirates would thus become a "one-stop shop" for travel, and a digital hybrid itself.

As digital technology is increasingly determining the future of every company's business and is therefore becoming a central and strategic element of every company, across all industries and sectors, executives must become increasingly aware of how best to leverage digitalisation and digital transformation to ensure that their company remains relevant.

3

The strategic
role of IT

The following section explores the role of IT and the CIO in companies that are undergoing digitalisation and/or digital transformation. For the sake of simplicity, I will use the term CIO to indicate individuals in a company who are responsible for information technology (IT). Depending on the organisation, the appropriate title might be Chief Digital Officer (CDO), Chief Technology Officer (CTO), Head of IT, Chief Technology and Information Officer (CTIO), or Chief Digital Information Officer (CDIO), but this is irrelevant for our purposes.

In most companies, the CIO's role is traditionally still viewed as a support function, not a source of value creation. IT supports the core business by automating routine processes and by providing tools and applications to the employees who work on value creation. However, this positioning of IT has changed significantly in most of the forward-thinking companies, because in most industries and companies, IT has become an integral part of products and services, even if traditional managers do not always realise it or do not want to realise it. Particularly in sectors where no physical goods are delivered to the customer, such as banks and insurance companies, IT has become a central element of the product.

When technology – and in particular IT – becomes an integral and strategic part of the value-creation process, it can no longer be treated as a mere support function delegated to a CIO who focuses mainly on running the back office. Technology is now an important strategic component of the company's core business, and therefore, the person responsible for IT in the company - let's assume this is still the CIO - will have to play a different and much more strategic role than in the past. Some of the traditional ways of managing IT within a company will change drastically, as what worked well in the past may not succeed in the future.

Factors that shape the role of IT

I believe that several factors will strongly influence the future role of IT at the company level and thus the responsibilities and objectives of CIOs. This is not an exhaustive list, but it is a starting point for understanding how technology is transforming businesses:

- IT is no longer merely a support function but a strategic asset and the core of the business: a source of innovation and added value rather than a cost factor
- Convergence of process IT, production IT, and product IT
- Dematerialisation of physical objects: from hardware to software, driving software-defined products
- Open and technology-led innovation is increasingly pervasive
- Every leader must become a digital leader, or: "Who needs a CDO?"
- The days of centralised IT organisations are over, or: "Shadow IT, what's wrong with it?"
- Digital natives are entering the workforce, and networks are replacing hierarchies
- Shorter time-to-market cycles are required: everything must become agile
- Control over IT procurement is increasingly being transferred to users
- The make-or-buy discussion is back on the table
- Technology is becoming a topic for the board of directors

The future role of IT and the CIO

Convergence of product-IT & process-IT

From cost to value add

Technology becomes a key topic for boards of directors

From support function to strategic core of the business

Every leader becomes a digital leader

Core business has to take control over IT

Open and technology-driven innovation

Future of IT

Requirement for increasing agility -> Agile / DevOps

«Digital culture»: from hierarchies to network

Reverse outsourcing madness: in- & backsouroing

Dematerialization: from HW to SW, SW-defined products

Shadow IT: from curse to blessing

Increasing sourcing and control of technologies (HW & SW) by end-users

The impact of the factors listed above will lead to a number of changes that companies, and especially "traditional" CIOs or IT leaders, will need to think through carefully if they want to remain relevant in their companies. In my humble opinion, the only way for established CIOs to survive in their role is to drastically "disrupt" and reinvent themselves. If they don't do it, someone else will. The ongoing changes discussed in the following chapters are by no means an exhaustive list, but at this point they are clearly significant enough to call into question the traditional role of IT and the CIO.

From a support function to the core of the company

Technological change has always brought immense opportunities. Technology has not only enabled increases in productivity in every imaginable industry, but it has also helped create entirely new industries and transformed established ones. For innovative individuals and companies, one of the greatest sources of inspiration for innovation has always been to closely examine technological achievements and consider their possible commercial applications. Very often, the real potential and value of a new technology is discovered only decades after its invention. It is therefore worthwhile to examine new technologies and assess their possibilities at an early stage, even if one does not currently see any obvious opportunity to introduce them profitably in the short term.

When the transistor was invented at Bell Laboratories in Murray Hill, New Jersey in 1947, no one thought that it would eventually form the basis for the smartphones that each of us now, almost 80 years later, carries around every day and that have revolutionised our entire society. Without this semiconductor technology, our way of living would be radically different. Today, our entire lives and society are largely founded on achievements and products based on this technology. Total semiconductor sales have increased exponentially in recent decades, rising from US$14.7 billion in 1982 to US$149 billion in 1999 and reaching a record US$556 billion in 2021.[2] Moreover, these sales represent only the direct value generated by the semiconductor industry. If all the industries and products that are based on semiconductor technology

---

2   Semiconductor Industry Association and World Semiconductor Trade Statistics (https://www.wsts.org)

were included, we would be talking about orders of magnitude that I would not even dare to estimate.

Similarly, when the Wright brothers attempted the first powered flight in December 1903 – it was actually more of a 37-metre hop that lasted just 12 seconds – no one would have thought that the first commercial airline for passenger transport would take off only ten years later, marking the birth of a whole new industry. Today, after recovering from the COVID-19 pandemic, the aviation industry is once again among the fastest-growing transport sectors in an increasingly interconnected global economy. In 2023, its market volume was estimated at just under US$815 billion, only around 3 per cent below its 2019 level.

Technology is part of the product

Innovative companies are constantly scanning the market for technologies that might help them improve, complement, or create new products or services, make processes more efficient, or eliminate process steps or even entire processes. As noted above, for a long time traditional companies predominantly used IT to increase efficiency, automate processes, and optimise supply chains. Only in rare cases did IT find its way into their core products and services, and often it only did so at a much later stage, with the exception of technology companies, of course.

To cite another example from the aviation industry, in the early 1950s American Airlines introduced the first electronic booking system to optimise its internal processes and better manage the inventory of available seats between its sales offices. However, it would take another 50 years before airline passengers could seamlessly access up-to-date information on their flight electronically, check the availability and

December 1903

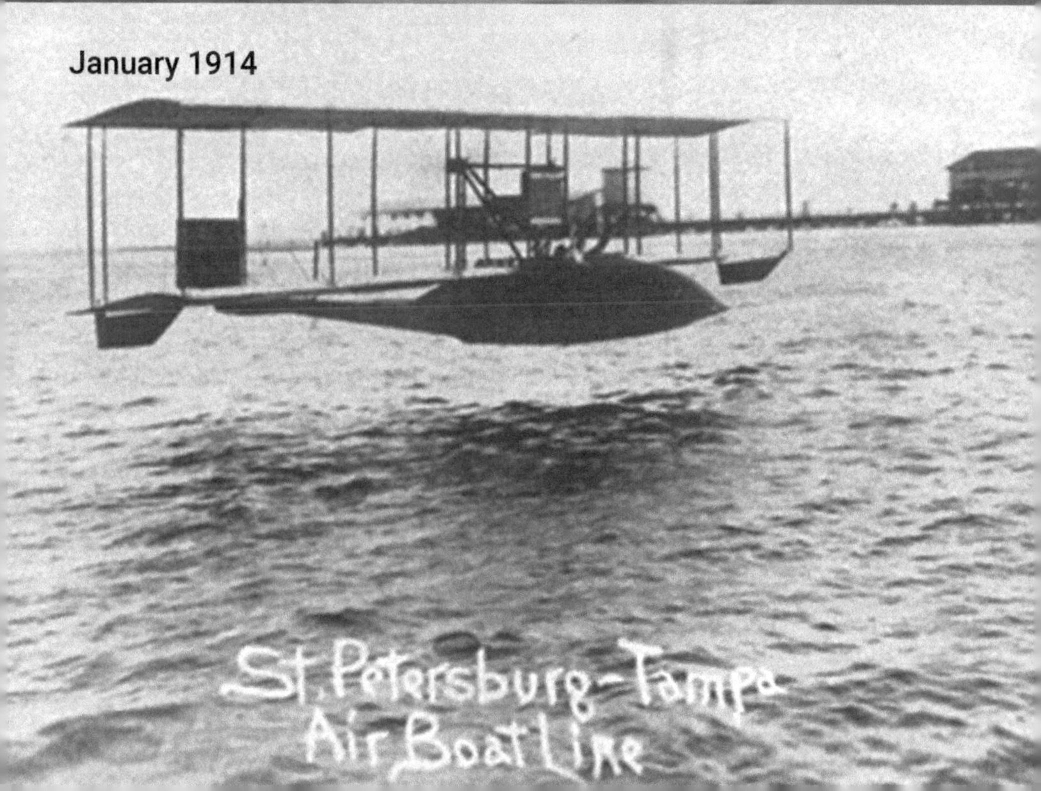

January 1914

St.Petersburg-Tampa
Air Boat Line

current prices of flights online, or book their flights themselves. Even today, uptake of these services is still not universal, but many travellers now use a mobile app to access up-to-date travel information throughout the journey, check in at the airport, or book additional products and services (e.g., seat selection, extra luggage, etc.). Moreover, airline customers consider the availability of such apps to be part of the product or service offered by an airline. Onboard technology is also becoming increasingly interactive and personalised, as travellers are now able to connect their smartphones, tablets, and other devices directly to the in-flight entertainment system, allowing them to stream their own content on the large display screen, display films and information provided by the airline on their own devices, or listen to airline-provided content (music, podcasts, audiobooks etc.) using their own headphones. IT has thus become as much a part of the product (the travel experience) as the seat, the food, and service onboard the aircraft, which was not the case before 2010.

When I joined Emirates Airlines in Dubai as CIO at the beginning of 2006, hardly anyone saw IT as part of the airline's core product, and customer expectations were very different to what they are today. Although my former employer, Swissair, had offered flight bookings via its website as early as 1997, this sales channel had for many years remained little used, with only the most tech-savvy early adopters going online to book a flight. Just a few years after my first day at Emirates Airlines, we introduced the first version of a mobile app. Today, this app is as indispensable as the onboard entertainment system, good service, and decent food on long-haul flights – at least on quality airlines such as Emirates.

Similarly, for the owner of a modern electric car, digital interaction is as much a part of the product as any physical component, as drivers expect downloadable upgrades and product-enhancement options. As more and more functions and features of a physical product move into the software – in other words, they are being virtualised (see the chapter on virtualisation) – and additional digital services are offered in order to complement the product and improve functionality and user experience, IT itself becomes a core part of the product.

The replacement or combination of traditional physical products and services with digital and virtual components means that IT can no longer be considered merely a support or back-office function. IT is responsible for far more than merely operating process-automation systems such as the ERP system or managing end-user devices and networks. IT is becoming a core element of every company, and its role is far more strategic than supportive. As a result, IT should no longer be viewed purely as a cost factor. On the contrary, it now contributes to the core value-creation of products and services and generates revenue.

Companies such as Tesla recognised very early on the possibility of extending the performance and functionality of their vehicles via software upgrades, even long after the vehicle has already been delivered to the customer. A new Tesla model is often essentially just a software upgrade. The owner does not even have to take the car to a mechanic or dealership, because the upgrades can be downloaded and installed directly "over the air" on the vehicle. Whereas cars used to deteriorate every year after delivery, falling further and further behind the newest models on the market, a car with a large share of upgradeable software components can actually improve its functionality over time and keep pace with latest developments. A vehicle that has been delivered to a customer is therefore never really "finished", as a traditional car manufacturer would understand the term, because the production process continues over the entire lifespan of the vehicle.

Cost factor or added value

In the past, as mentioned above, most companies treated IT primarily as a cost component, and the CIO's performance was measured largely in terms of his or her ability to reduce IT cost. CIOs of the future, however, will need to focus on how IT creates added value for the company by enhancing its core products and services, generating revenue, and improving the customer experience. Today, the CIO's performance is increasingly measured by the added value of IT and no longer just by costs.

This new mandate, in turn, requires CIOs to become more strategic and business-focused in their thinking. A modern CIO must be more entrepreneurial and less operational, i.e. less risk averse and less cost oriented. CIOs who fail to make this leap, court the danger of becoming increasingly irrelevant and may end up managing legacy IT systems and infrastructure, essentially devolving into "Chief Legacy Officers".

Convergence of product technology, production technology, and process technology

Most companies maintain a strict separation between responsibilities for product technology, production technology, and process IT. Product technology is technology that forms part of the products and services produced and offered by the company. Production technology (also called operational technology) is the technology used to automate and control production facilities and machines in manufacturing (e.g., CNC, SCADA, etc.), including technologies associated with Industry 4.0. Process IT, on the other hand, is the technology used to automate and optimise internal and external processes such as ERP systems, supply chain management, and sales systems, etc. Typically, the CIO is responsible for process IT and the company's IT infrastructure, while someone else (product development, the CTO, etc.) is responsible for product technology, and yet another person (often the COO) is responsible for production technology.

As product technology and production technology get more and more digitalised (e.g., with IoT products, software-defined products, sensors in production, etc.), it is becoming increasingly difficult, if not impossible, to separate process, product, and production IT. As a result, close interaction and coordination among these three areas is essential, especially since they often use the same technologies. The methods and patterns used in process IT must be adapted to product technology and production technology, including the ability to interact with software-based products and provide updates, upgrades, and/or cybersecurity support well after delivery to the customer.

A good example of this necessity is the car manufacturer Tesla, which we have already mentioned in the previous chapter. Tesla recognised that its vehicles are not "finished" products when they leave the assembly line but must be continually updated and therefore constantly connected to product life-cycle management system (PLM) via the back-end ERP system. The shift from hardware to more software components (and ultimately software-defined products) reinforces this effect. For Tesla, a new model is often simply a software upgrade, and customers can purchase additional performance and features online (e.g., unlocking additional battery capacity, improved motor performance, etc.), immediately obtaining additional functionality for their vehicle. This option is becoming an important source of revenue for Tesla and is a key part of its business model.

However, Tesla also had to realise that the traditional ERP system and its product life-cycle modules were only suitable for controlling and managing product development and vehicle production when those vehicles were still physically at the production site. Once a vehicle had been delivered to the customer, the ERP system ceased to be suitable even though Tesla vehicles are never in their "finished" state and are actually "in production" throughout their entire life-cycle. Tesla recognised that connecting customers' vehicles to their production system over the entire lifespan of the vehicle represented a strategic competitive advantage, but none of the established providers of ERP systems were able to support this functionality. Tesla therefore declared the ERP system and most of the other IT systems to be strategic components of the company and a competitive advantage that they did not want to share with rival companies and began developing a fully integrated ERP system from scratch. When the company bosses of the established ERP suppliers in Walldorf or Silicon Valley heard about this move, they must have wondered, "Who on earth comes up with the idea of developing an ERP themselves these days?"

These developments show that the era of separating product, production, and process IT is over. With digitalisation of products and concepts of Industry 4.0, these disciplines are converging into an inseparable whole. As a result, the traditional division of responsibilities, in which the CIO's mandate covers process IT, while a CTO is responsible for product technology, and a COO is tasked with overseeing production technology, will disappear. The CIO of the future will either succeed in becoming the individual who also drives IT-based product and production innovation or be relegated to looking after elements of the remaining physical infrastructure and the old back-end systems.

A business-focused CIO who also drives the company's digital agenda, including the design, creation, innovation, and digitalisation of products and services, will move out of the back office and into the core of the products and services. A stronger focus on using strategic technology as an enabler for new business models, products, and services – as well as a means of optimising and increasing production efficiency and promoting innovation through technology – will be critical to the CIO of the future.

However, this new breed of CIO will also need to work and think in network terms rather than solely in terms of traditional hierarchical systems. What counts in networked structures is neither reporting lines nor the number of employees that a CIO oversees, but the influence they can exert on the company and its success, as well as the added value they can create for the company.

6

The virtualisation of "things"

My wife is a very organised person. For the past 20 years or so, she has drawn up checklists of what we will take with us when we go travelling. There are lists for skiing holidays, diving holidays, city trips, etc., on which everything is meticulously itemised so that we do not forget anything important.

Recently, I looked through these lists and realised that we no longer carry many of these items, such as photo cameras, film reels, alarm clocks, torches, books, tour guides, travel tickets, cash, credit cards, music players, and games, with us as physical objects when we travel.

If you take stock of all the physical objects that we used only two decades ago, you will see that many of them have literally disappeared. They no longer have a physical form but now exist only as data or services in the cloud or as an app on a smartphone or tablet. This trend towards the virtualisation and dematerialisation of physical objects is not only something that we notice every day in our private lives, but it has had – or will have – a fundamental impact on how most businesses operate. While some sectors, such as the music and photography industries, have already experienced these effects, many other companies have yet to come to terms with them.

Only a decade ago, most music was still sold and distributed on physical media such as CDs, cassettes, and vinyl records. Today, the overwhelming majority of music is sold, streamed, or downloaded from online platforms. While vinyl retains an enduring appeal, most forms of physical music media – and the stores that used to sell them – have all but disappeared. Moreover, digital business models for music sales have also evolved, with subscription services largely replacing the sale of individual tracks or albums. Members of the younger generation, my daughter included, do not understand why a person would buy single tracks or albums when they could stream music from a vast library, unlimited and any time you want, with a Spotify subscription.

The virtualisation of objects drops the marginal cost of reproducing them almost to zero. Distribution is effectively instantaneous, as are updates and upgrades. The shift from the physical to the virtual world has enormous implications for businesses. Twenty years ago, photographs were most often developed manually and delivered to customers on physical paper. Today, photo printing and distribution have largely disappeared, and photos are overwhelmingly digital and distributed electronically. Video recorders are likewise virtual, and videos can be stored, edited, and streamed from the cloud via a subscription service like Zattoo. A timer, alarm clock, stopwatch, calculator, and even a small torch is now available for free on every smartphone. Digital music in MP3 or FLAC format no longer requires an iPod or other dedicated devices and can now be played on any smartphone or computer. Digital music files can also be copied and distributed indefinitely (if we ignore the issue of copyright for a moment). Storage space for digital photos is available in huge quantities on our devices or in the cloud and is practically free. Free digital maps on our smartphones or tablet computers have replaced physical maps on paper. They are not only much more up to date than printed maps but also offer much greater functionality (plus, you no longer have to deal with the hassle of folding them). The camera industry has changed drastically because hardly anyone buys a physical camera anymore, as most mobile phones offer a combination of high-quality photo and video cameras. The camera industry has been marginalised to focus on a small niche of professional or specialist devices (e.g., GoPro action cams) or devices based on novelty or nostalgia (e.g., Polaroid).

My hypothesis is that any object that captures or collects information (e.g., a camera or microphone), stores information (e.g., a book, film

Virtualisation (digitisation) of 'things'

reel, music cassette, CD, or DVD), processes information (e.g., a calculator or language translator) or displays information (e.g., a watch, ticket, credit card, or ID document) has the potential to be dematerialised or virtualised into an app or a service in the cloud or on our smartphone and will therefore gradually cease to exist as a physical thing.

An extremely important but often overlooked property of virtual objects in the digital world is their mutual connectivity. Apps and other virtualised objects can be connected to each other and exchange data, i.e. they can share information with each other: an electronic airline ticket in my digital wallet can communicate with the calendar and alarm clock on my mobile phone, helping ensure that I do not miss my flight. The GPS on my mobile phone can connect with a digital travel guide, helping me navigate an unfamiliar city with ease. Various virtual objects are increasingly combining information, and they often do so automatically, with no input from the user, such as when a smartphone uses its GPS to geotag photos.

As Google Maps, Apple Maps, Waze, and other smartphone apps have become ubiquitous, dedicated car navigation systems with their own physical devices, – you may still remember the Garmin or TomTom devices that you could install in your car – have largely disappeared. Most car manufacturers, however, continue to install their own navigation systems in their vehicles, even though hardly anyone uses them anymore, since the information from navigation apps on a mobile phone connected to the onboard infotainment hub of the car is much more up-to-date and accurate, and navigation apps typically also offer far more functions than any car manufacturer's built-in navigation system. In addition, smartphone navigation apps link with other data sources to increase their functionality and enrich the information displayed. For example, addresses stored in contacts or destinations searched in Google can be displayed on the Google Maps mobile app. While these networks of virtual objects are increasingly common, their potential is

Every **physical object** that:

⇒ **acquires**

⇒ **stores**

⇒ **manipulates**

⇒ **displays**

Information, has the

potential to be

dematerialised/

virtualised

Patrick Naef

far from exhausted, and they offer companies a fantastic opportunity for innovation and optimisation.

Marc Andreesen,[3] co-inventor of the graphical Internet browser Mosaic, founder of Netscape, and today a successful venture capitalist and investor in technology startups, foresaw the growing virtualisation of objects when he made his famous statement in 2011: *"Software is eating the world"*. This is exactly what is happening today: through dematerialisation, hardware (physical objects) is transitioning into software. What could already be observed in the computer industry and has long been referred to as "software-defined" is now expanding into all areas and "software-defined" products are emerging, offering all the advantages discussed in previous chapters. To return to the automotive industry, cars are increasingly becoming software-defined vehicles. Tesla exemplifies this process, but the trend is evident across manufacturers.

As I have now mentioned Tesla several times, I would like to allow myself a short digression to clarify an important point. I am by no means a "Tesla fan", and I do not drive a Tesla myself, though I do drive an electric car. However, I do credit Tesla for practically re-inventing the car, along with its manufacturing and sales process, through the creative and consistent application of modern technologies. Tesla has pioneered much of what other car manufacturers are doing today. However, I also struggle with the personality cult surrounding Tesla founder Elon Musk and with Tesla's attempts to create a monopoly using proprietary technology and service restrictions. A few years ago, I tried to charge my electric car at a Tesla fast-charging station and was shocked to realise that only Tesla vehicles could be charged there (at least at the time that was the case). It would be as if France's Elf-Total allowed only Renault vehicles to refuel at their petrol stations. If this were to catch on, every manufacturer would have to set up its own charging network, which would be

---

3   https://en.wikipedia.org/wiki/Marc_Andreessen

disastrous both ecologically and economically. Tesla's approach, however, is similar to Apple's strategy for proprietary technology, which will be discussed in a later chapter.

Attempts to digitalise companies' business processes that fail to account for dematerialisation tend to be as short-sighted as those that automate only traditional processes that are still focused on physical objects. Companies aiming at substantially redesigning or even re-inventing processes need to think beyond the world of physical objects and imagine a situation dominated by apps, networks, and computer programs, in which most physical objects are virtualised. For example, when airlines replace their check-in counters with self-service kiosks, they fail to recognise that in a digitalised world, where neither tickets nor boarding passes exist in physical forms, tickets no longer need to be exchanged for boarding passes – eliminating the need for a manual check-in process altogether – which today is becoming increasingly common. While luggage tags can now be printed and attached at home, luggage itself must still be checked in physically. According to my hypothesis, however, even this step will soon disappear, because the luggage tag is nothing more than a physical object that stores and displays information (in the form of printed numbers, letters and bar codes) and therefore has the potential to be virtualised. The start-up BagsID,[4] for example, has developed a technology that uniquely identifies luggage without bar codes or RFID tags, on a purely optical basis using sophisticated AI algorithms analysing video feeds; a kind of "biometric impression" of the luggage item. If we humans can recognise our luggage among all the rest based on its size, colour, scratches, dents, stickers, and other characteristics, then an AI algorithm can certainly do the same, and most probably with even greater reliability. Moreover, the technology can utilise existing CCTV feeds and cheap cameras, obviating the need for expensive and often unreliable barcode scanners.

---

4   https://www.bagsid.com

Banks have replaced some of their counter staff with cashpoints (ATMs), but this is only a first step to reduce costs. The actual breakthrough for bank customers will come once money itself has been fully virtualised and paper banknotes are no longer used. A fully cashless society appeared impossible to many of us just a few years ago, but during the COVID-19 pandemic electronic payments suddenly replaced a large share of cash transactions. Cash is fundamentally no different than many of the other physical objects that have been virtualised in recent years. A banknote or a coin is also just a physical object to store and display information and is merely a promise of "value" in the exchange process, and that information can be digitised, eliminating the need for the physical object.

The music industry has had to learn painful lessons about failing to properly leverage technology in time in order to benefit from new digital products, distribution channels, and business models. As a lifelong music lover, when I visited the United States in the 1980s I enjoyed spending hours in the big music stores like Tower Records and Virgin, browsing their seemingly endless shelves in search of rare records of my favourite jazz musicians. At the turn of the millennium, however, we saw the arrival of the digital revolution, and everything changed. Everything? Well, not exactly. It is true that vinyl records were replaced by CDs, and VHS video cassettes were replaced by DVDs. The products thus became digitised, but the distribution model had barely changed. CDs were still sold in physical music stores, just like cassette tapes and just like eight-track tapes and vinyl records before them. Yet within a decade, these music stores had largely disappeared, and most had gone bankrupt. What had happened?

New entrants to this market, such as Spotify, Deezer, and Apple's iTunes service, capitalised on the opportunity to distribute music digitally. Within just a few years, new business models such as subscription streaming services have come to dominate the music industry, and you

New Business Models

Music Store 1980 **Music Store 2000** **Music Store 2010**

Music Store 2010

iTunes **Google Play Music** **Spotify** **Deezer**

no longer need to buy the music but instead can stream it whenever you like. When iTunes was first established, Apple initially used it to continue selling music downloads, but this approach miserably failed. When streaming subscription services such as Spotify and Deezer tapped into the zeitgeist of the younger generation with their "sharing mindset", they seized a large share of the iTunes customer base. Ultimately, Apple was left with no option other than to adopt a subscription model as well.

Meanwhile, the traditional music chains with their prestigious stores in prime locations suddenly found themselves with hardly any customers. Digitised music no longer needed to be sold in the traditional way, on physical media, but could now be streamed much more easily, efficiently, faster and cheaper over the Internet, as Spotify and Deezer were doing. Music had been almost entirely virtualised. For members of the younger generation – like my daughter – it is hard to imagine having to buy and own music on physical media or even having to possess your own music files when you can stream music at will via Spotify.

Leaders who want to use IT to create sustainable, significant added value for their companies must go beyond simply aiming to achieve short-term cost savings by automating established processes while continuing to rely on the existing physical objects, as this is merely the low-hanging fruit of digitalisation. Instead, they should adopt a more far-sighted approach that focuses on technology-driven innovation, recognising that most of the objects that collect, store, process, and display data no longer exist in a physical form – they are now virtualised. Rather than clinging to physical objects that make their processes slow, cumbersome, and expensive, CIOs should work closely with their business colleagues across departments to exploit the potential of dematerialisation.

Open innovation

Given the rapid pace with which new technologies are coming to market, the traditional approach of driving innovation solely from within the company is becoming increasingly difficult to sustain. Internal company regulations, processes, control frameworks, and organisational structures are slowing down innovation and are paralysing the organisation. Some of the biggest innovation killers are traditional financial processes, such as budgeting and business cases. If you look at the greatest innovations of the last few decades, how many do you think were underpinned by a solid financial business case? Probably not even one.

It is still common in most companies to request technology and innovation budgets via the regular annual budget process, while a prospective investment in an innovation project that exceeds a certain threshold must be accompanied by a detailed business case demonstrating its potential profitability. After estimating the total cost of the project, the applicant must convince the Chief Financial Officer (CFO) that the investment is profitable. Only then will the funding be released. This approach is appropriate for investments in traditional infrastructure, with known costs and easily quantifiable benefits, but it is not at all suitable for investments in innovation.

Releasing funds gradually and in stages, starting with a modest amount, would enable research teams to experiment while the stakes are still low. *"Fail, but fail fast and cheap"* is a motto in Silicon Valley, one of the world's greatest innovation centres. It suggests that the best approach is to conduct a wide range of experiments, but to quickly stop those that are not promising and then try something else. Such failures are not setbacks but learning experiences. The money that was spent is not lost if the experiment is abandoned, but; it is the cost of the organisational learning and experience gained during the experiment, because it contributes to a body of knowledge that generates value in the long term. Companies should book these expenditures as costs, not as capital investments. If funding is allocated to innovation projects in the traditional way, the temptation for managers is to try to get the largest possible budget at the beginning so that they need not return to the CFO to ask for more money. In my experience, any allocated resources will almost certainly be spent, and I have very rarely seen a project return unused funds. However, the worst element of the traditional approach is that funds devoted to innovation are capitalised and therefore treated as an investment. If it becomes apparent that the innovation in question will not be successful, but funds are still available, it is a safe bet that the project will nevertheless continue until the money has been used up. Because the sum involved is now quite large and sits on the balance sheet as an investment, the manager will not want to cancel it, as that would require writing off the entire investment as a loss. A manager in this position will often opt to apply for even more funds, hence "throwing good money after bad" under the guise of "investment protection", to protect an "investment" with little hope of success.

True innovation requires 'out-of-the-box' thinking, which employees with day-to-day operational tasks are often unable to apply to the necessary extent. Tapping into the innovation ecosystems of start-ups, the open-source community, universities, research labs, and venture capital firms can be a far more efficient way to expand the pool of innovative ideas far beyond what one's own employees would normally be able to contribute. Most employees in operational functions tend to focus solely on incremental improvements and ideas that represent "more of the same, but better". There is a famous quote attributed to Henry Ford, the automotive pioneer and founder of the Ford Motor Company, which in 1908 launched the first car to be produced on an assembly line, the Model T: *"If I had asked people what they wanted, they*

Open, Connected, Shared & Crowd Sourcing

That's where innovation happens.

The way of working of the younger generation.

Accept that users and customers will be in control.

The more you share, the more you will receive.

Open Architectures: The times of monolithic systems are over.

Open up the company for collaboration, be part of it!

Adapt OpenSource community models.

Shorter, iterative and agile development cycles.

Patrick Naef

would have said faster horses". By 1918, almost every other car in America was a Ford Model T.

As more products and services are digitised, technology increasingly sets the pace for innovation and therefore also defines the speed with which new product innovations can be brought to market. I believe that most companies will not be able to innovate fast enough if they continue to rely solely on their own internal resources. Technological innovations in particular require a different approach than the traditional, in-house innovation funnel of own ideas or the traditional internal suggestion box. Open innovation requires companies to open their products and services, make application programming interfaces (APIs) available to partners or the public, disclose their software codes, and encourage the open-source community to contribute and co-develop additional features and components that enhance and improve the company's core products and services. As open innovation potentially allows the whole world to help drive innovation, it is essential to overcome the limitations imposed by the existing technology.

This is exactly what Google and Apple have done with their smartphone ecosystems. It is not the smartphone itself or the operating system that represents the device's added value, but the apps developed by independent developers, which users can install and configure themselves. This approach has enabled Apple and Google to draw on thousands of top-class developers, whose apps extend and improve the functionality of their devices, personalise them for the user, and contribute to the value of the larger ecosystem and hence of the device. Apple almost missed this opportunity by adhering to the philosophy of a closed ecosystem. The first versions of the iPhone were delivered with only pre-installed apps, and it was impossible to install apps from other sources, manufacturers, or developers. Steve Jobs believed that he could meet all his customers' needs with the pre-installed apps.

Google, meanwhile, pursued a completely different path with its open Android system, namely that of an open ecosystem. When Android developed rapidly thanks to its open concept, threatening Apple's position in the smartphone market, Apple was compelled to give in and open up the iPhone ecosystem to third-party apps. However, Apple remains much more restrictive than Google – allegedly due to security concerns – about what apps can be installed on their devices (yes, Apple considers every iPhone to be *their* device, even though you as the user have bought it). Until recently, apps could be downloaded only from Apple's own app store unless users unlocked (jailbreak) their iPhones and risked voiding the warranty. It was only when the EU began applying pressure to comply with the relevant laws and regulations that Apple was forced to allow apps from third-party marketplaces on iPhones. Nevertheless, downloading MP3 music files that were not purchased from Apple's iTunes store remains almost impossible for a normal user, whereas with Android it could not be simpler.

Another issue that comes with a closed system like Apple's are proprietary connectors. When we go on holiday as a family, my wife and I can charge all of our devices (Android smartphone, tablet, e-reader, earphones, Bluetooth speaker, laptop, underwater camera, fitness band, etc.) with a single standard USB-C cable. Our daughter, on the other hand, always needs at least two charging cables – one for her iPhone and a second for all her other devices. Fortunately, the EU authorities have recently obliged Apple to offer the standard USB-C connector on all of its new devices.

Corporate venture funds have long since discovered that investing in start-ups outside of their company can drive innovation without the constraints imposed by internal processes, regulations, or other limitations. Working closely with the innovation ecosystem in technology hotspots such as Silicon Valley, London's Silicon Roundabout, or the Berlin technology scene greatly increases the potential for really innovative ideas to reach fruition. Collaboration with independent venture capital firms, incubators, and universities can further contribute to and accelerate the innovation process.

During my time at Emirates Airlines, we began to build our own innovation ecosystem, shortly after I joined. What started with a modest innovation lab established in cooperation with Microsoft in 2008 grew over the years into a real engine for innovation. We established a second innovation lab in Silicon Valley with Carnegie Mellon University (CMU), founded a data-science lab in England with Oxford University, and organised multiple hackathons in various locations every year, with at least one always being held in Silicon Valley. Each hackathon was also sponsored by a business unit – in addition to me as CIO – and the unit posed a real-life challenge as the hackathon task. For these hackathons, we also provided APIs of the systems (not to the operational systems, of course, but of the test environment) and data used by the respective business unit.

Several of the solutions that were developed during a hackathon were later expanded into operational products and put into production. We also organised in-house hackathons and formed an internal community of developers, which included pilots and flight attendants who developed innovative apps in their spare time. This community resulted in the creation of 35 apps in a single year, most of which were subsequently rolled out operationally. We simply provided the infrastructure, APIs, and any licences required for their development.

In 2011, we were honoured with the "Innovation of the Year Award" for creating one of the first company-internal app stores. Ironically, this prize was awarded by one of the leading smartphone companies at the time, which itself then missed the boat on innovation and as a result is now barely clinging to relevancy – namely, BlackBerry (RIM).

Our innovation lab in Silicon Valley enabled us to work closely with universities and engage with the start-up scene. I sat on advisory boards of various leading venture capital firms. We collaborated with a wide variety of start-ups, conducted experiments with innovative technologies, and were at the forefront of the industry in areas such as AI/ML, blockchain, beacons, digital twins, IoT, AR/VR and many more. While not all of those technologies proved a success, or succeeded only partially at getting implemented by the company, the costs of exploring them were practically negligible compared to the added value that we generated from them, because we applied the principle of *"fail, but fail fast and cheap"* and learnt a lot as an organisation. Moreover, many of these experiments with new technologies were co-financed by large technology companies who were very interested in how the results would be applied in the real world by a market leader such as Emirates Airlines, which helped keep our costs low. Innovation through experimentation does not have to be expensive.

If the CIOs of tomorrow want to be seen as leaders who drive innovation through technology, they must focus on applying the most diverse, open innovation techniques in collaboration with partners in the broader innovation ecosystem. This approach could include organising hackathons, regularly participating in "speed-dating" sessions with technology start-ups, joining the advisory boards of venture capital firms, or sponsoring research projects at leading universities. I believe that in our networked and open world, the days of secretive, isolated corporate research labs are a thing of the past.

Every leader must be a digital leader, or: "Who needs a CDO?"

When digitalisation and the digital transformation became hot topics a few years ago, many companies that did not know how to get to grips with the topic, or whose CIOs were overwhelmed by the complex challenge involved, simply appointed a Chief Digital Officer (CDO) in the hope that this new executive would solve their digitalisation problems.

Technology is changing and defining the future of every company, and as a result it has become one of the most important strategic factors for almost any business, on par with human resources and financial resources. However, while every manager is expected to know how to deal with employees and financial resources, it is still widely accepted that technology issues can be delegated to a separate entity or person, as many managers still lack the necessary competencies or the confidence to engage with technology, while others are simply overwhelmed by it. Whether these responsibilities are delegated to a CTO, a CIO, or a CDO, the pattern is the same: technology is not considered a strategic factor or a key component of the core business, and as such it can be delegated to a specific person or support department. Very often, this person reports to the Chief Financial Officer (CFO), as IT is perceived as a cost factor. With the growing drive towards digitalisation, many companies have tried to fill this gap by hiring a CDO.

CDOs are hired to drive a company's digital agenda, but many have attempted to build administrative fiefdoms of their own. The reason for this approach is that most of these "experienced leaders" are still traditional, hierarchical managers who lack the flexibility and open-mindedness required to engage effectively with the digital and networked world. As a result, they often attempt to build a discrete digital business unit that offers digital products and services to the market that are separate from the established business lines. This can lead to competition with the traditional business units, creating unnecessary internal friction that paralyses the company through massive internal politics instead of improving its competitive position in the market.

However, there is a growing acceptance that IT has become an important strategic component of every company, and that organisation-wide digitalisation is necessary for companies to remain competitive. As a result, we can see today that the age of the CDO is over. Most companies are distancing themselves from the entire concept of the CDO, as they have recognised that digitalisation cannot be established as a standalone discipline with its own organisation that exists apart from, and often competes with, the traditional business. While well-established, business-oriented CIOs can act as enablers and catalysts for digitalisation to help their business colleagues become more digital, every executive ultimately needs to become a "digital leader" in their own right. IT is so strategic to every major company that responsibility for technology can no longer be delegated to a CIO or CDO and must instead be anchored in the core business.

I have been working in executive search for six years now, and I have helped dozens of companies find the right leaders for IT. We often work with the client to develop the job profile before we begin looking for suitable candidates. However, I have never been asked to search for a CDO. In the vast majority of cases, the search profile has developed in the direction of a combined CDIO (Chief Digital and Information Officer) role, but with a strong focus on transferring responsibility for digitalisation topics to the relevant business leader and with the CDIO acting as a coach and catalyst for digitalisation and business development from the perspective of the company as a whole.

It's impossible to be an **effective leader** unless you are also an effective **digital leader.**

In recent years, many articles have been published about the new "CxO" roles that were invented and introduced as soon as topic "x" became strategically relevant for a company. The major consulting firms in particular, whose consultants have usually never held relevant leadership positions in large companies themselves, recommend that their clients create such new CxO positions. The German car manufacturer Volkswagen introduced a Chief Software Officer at the beginning of 2019 because it recognised that dematerialization was progressively replacing hardware with software, making software increasingly strategic for the business. In the meantime, however, the role of the Chief Software Officer at VW has been eliminated. Other companies, recognising the importance of networking and digitalising their products, introduced Chief IoT Officer, others introduced a Chief Transformation Officer, a Chief Innovation Officer, or a Chief Data Officer to fill the apparent "gap" in their organisations.

As this trend closely follows the latest high-profile technology, many firms are now considering introducing a Chief AI Officer. Of course, AI technology will ultimately affect all companies, and every executive should consider the impact it will have on their business, as well as how it can be used to improve efficiency and strengthen competitive positioning. But to create a new C-suite position for this is, in my humble opinion, excessive at best and wasteful at worst. Likewise, I would consider it wasteful to create a Chief Data Officer position, despite the obvious importance of data to all aspects of a company. AI, like software and data, is part of information technology (IT), and if the CIO fails to devote sufficient focus and attention to these topics and does not treat them sufficiently as strategic elements for the business, it is probably time to retire the CIO and find someone who can handle the responsibilities that the position today requires.

It seems that whenever an existing C-suite executive is not doing their job properly or is stuck in the past, the solution is simply to create a new CxO role to fill the gap, rather than asking whether the existing executives are in fact aware of the most important issues facing the company and capable of addressing them. If a company is struggling to hire enough professionals and bring talents on board, the problem is that the Chief People Officer is failing to deliver the human resources that the company needs, and thus the solution is not to create a new "Chief Recruitment Officer" position. If the CFO is not handling the budget process effectively, hiring a "Chief Budgeting Officer" will not resolve that issue. The company must take the necessary actions to ensure that the CFO is able to do their job properly or begin looking for a new CFO. By creating new C-suite positions, a firm risks ending up with a whole plethora of CxOs while still failing to revise its expectations for corporate leaders in the digital age.

If a business-oriented CIO is able to drive the digital agenda, promote innovation through technology, enable the organisation to use technology as a competitive advantage, build the required digital skills and competencies as a core element of the business, support colleagues in cultivating digital leadership, and learn how to lead in network structures, then there is no need for a CDO. Indeed, if a company hires a CDO, this indicates to me that the CIO is not doing their job properly – at least, not the job that is expected of a modern, business focussed, forward-thinking CIO. In most cases, however, an outdated CIO job description that has hardly been revised for decades fails to adequately reflect the requirements of the CIO's new roles and responsibilities. The requirements for holding the increasingly vital position of CIO must change to reflect the company's needs to thrive in the digital age. Otherwise, CIOs – just like CDOs – will soon be relegated to the history books as business units themselves become more digital and technology-savvy.

Shadow IT: A solution disguised as a problem

For decades, CIOs have been fighting shadow IT organisations in their companies. The widespread view has been that everything related to IT must be controlled and managed centrally by the CIO and their IT organisation. This approach was justified by security and risk aspects, cost optimisation, avoidance of duplication, standardisation, and other rationales. Although costs could probably be optimised by centralising IT responsibilities, the downside was that speed, innovation, and proximity to the business, and ultimately to customers, suffered under this approach. Shadow IT teams on the other hand are generally much closer to the business – they are in fact completely integrated into the business – and usually understand the business, its requirements, and its customers better than centralised IT organisations do. They are also typically much faster and more agile in responding to changing market conditions, due to their smaller size and limited overhead.

Perhaps CIOs should see shadow IT teams as a blessing rather than a curse and be open to working with them rather than against them. The fact that business leaders are building, supporting, and defending shadow IT teams shows that they care about IT and see it as an essential and strategic component of their organisation – and that is not at all a bad thing.

I believe that the days of large, centralised IT organisations controlling all IT in the company are long gone. With the increasing digitalisation of businesses and their products and services, responsibility for IT and ownership of IT as a strategic part of the company must shift back to the business units, to the core of the business itself. Technological innovation should take place at all levels and be as close as possible to the business, not sequestered in an ivory tower at the corporate head-quarters, remote from the business. Therefore, shadow IT teams are best placed to innovate through technology, as they are literally at the core of the business.

However, simply decentralising IT functions back to business units represents a return to traditional, hierarchical structures – with their re-dundancies, inefficiencies, and incompatibilities – and thus it cannot be the solution. Instead, in the network age, we need to move away from traditional hierarchical structures and create a networked struc-ture of IT professionals throughout the entire company, where all staff work towards common goals and are driven by a common purpose rather than fussing over reporting lines. This structure is comparable to the way in which agile teams are organised and coordinated effective-ly. These teams consist of members from various organisational units (in the traditional, hierarchical sense), but they are driven by a com-mon purpose and work towards shared goals, which enables them to mostly organise and manage themselves without worrying too much about reporting lines and hierarchical company structures. However, this approach will work only if the transparency and visibility of these shadow IT teams within the company is ensured. As long as CIOs keep fighting these shadow IT units instead of embracing and collaborating with them, business leaders will try to hide these units and continue to call them "business support groups" or some similar euphemism de-signed to protect them from being subsumed under the authority of an old-fashioned, hierarchy-oriented CIO.

The role of the CIO must therefore change fundamentally. The CIO must move away from being the overseer of a centralised IT opera-tional unit and become more of a coach, catalyst, and networker who enables the company to transform itself into a digital enterprise. The CIO must also actively break loose from traditional hierarchical think-ing and serve as a role model for a networked organisation. It is not the size of the IT organisation, measured by its number of employees, or the size of the IT budget that defines the importance of IT and thus that of the CIO, but the added value that the CIO and IT bring to the company and the positive influence and impact that they exert on the company's stakeholders, i.e. the business, its employees, its customers, and the environment.

Collaborating closely with shadow IT teams across the entire company as part of a network can enable CIOs to benefit from their proximity and deep understanding of the business – as well as their flexibility, agility, and innovation power – without compromising standardisation, jeopardising security, increasing costs, or even drifting into uncontrolled chaos. I will discuss how this can be achieved in the chapter on network structures.

Shorter time-to-market cycles: Everything is becoming agile

"Agile" has become one of the most misused buzzwords of the past few years. Everything seems to be becoming agile, and everyone is claiming that they are agile. Have you ever heard someone say: "No, we are not agile"? But what do we really mean when we talk about agility in IT? The German-language Wikipedia article[5] on agile software development defines agile practices as follows:

"Agile software development (from the Latin agilis 'agile, flexible') refers to approaches in the software development process that are intended to increase transparency and the speed of change and lead to faster deployment of the developed system in order to minimise risks and erroneous developments in the development process. To this end, an attempt is made to reduce the design phase to a minimum and to achieve executable software as early as possible in the development process. This is harmonised with the customer at regular, short intervals. This should make it possible to respond flexibly to customer requests in order to increase overall customer satisfaction. Agile software development is characterised by self-organising teams and an iterative and incremental approach. Agile approaches can relate to parts of software development (e.g. agile modelling) or to the entire software development process (e.g. extreme programming or Scrum). The aim here is to make the development process more flexible and leaner than is the case with traditional, plan-driven process models (waterfall). Traditional approaches are often seen as heavyweight and bureaucratic (e.g. Rational Unified Process or V-model). One criticism levelled at them is that the more you work according to plan, the more you get what was planned, but not what is needed."

---

5   https://en.wikipedia.org/wiki/Agile_software_development

The concept of agile software development was popularised by the *"Manifesto for Agile Software Development"*[6], published in 2001, which describes its basic principles. The values and principles advocated by the manifesto were derived from a variety of software development frameworks, including Scrum, SAFe, and Kanban. The manifesto calls for an iterative approach to project management and software development that helps teams provide their customers with added value quickly and easily. Instead of releasing all its work at once in a single "big bang" launch package, an agile team delivers the results of its work in small, consumable increments. Requirements, plans, and results are continually evaluated so that the teams are able to react quickly to changes. Short, iterative cycles (sprints), streamlined administration, and the reduction of overhead and bureaucracy to a minimum are the essence of agility, as they allow the swift delivery of small portions of usable code that offer real added value for the business.

Minimising time to market is vital to competitiveness in today's business world, and the need to shorten time-to-market cycles is one of the main reasons that agile methods have become so popular. However, business managers often misunderstand agility and tend to see it as purely an "IT thing". They believe that introducing agile methods into their IT teams can allow projects of the same scope to be delivered faster and at a lower cost. This belief, however, is an illusion.

My personal experience as a CIO during an agile transformation has taught me that to truly benefit from agile methods the entire company must become agile. This process requires much more than merely the transformation of IT. It is not enough to implement a self-organisational management framework (i.e., Scrum) in IT, deliver a couple of projects using the agile approach, and believe that this framework will enable the company to react faster to market needs.

---

6   https://agilemanifesto.org/iso/de/manifesto.html

Agile Manifesto

Agile Values

We are uncovering **better ways of developing software by doing it and helping others do it.** Through this work we have come to value:

| Individuals and interactions | *over* | processes and tools |

| Working software | *over* | comprehensive documentation |

| Customer collaboration | *over* | contract negotiation |

| Responding to change | *over* | following a plan |

That is, while there is **value in the items on the right**, we **value the items on the left more.**

At Emirates Airlines, after years of using rapid prototyping methods and physically collocating our IT teams across business areas, we began introducing agile methods around 2013. This approach yielded benefits very quickly because we were able to develop and deliver smaller parts of ready-to-use software much faster than when using the traditional waterfall method. But when we wanted to put the code into production, we were stuck with our own IT-internal, ITIL-based processes. Our IT operations colleagues, who were responsible for safeguarding the "holy grail" of stable and secure operation, allowed only new or modified software code to be released into production at pre-defined times based on stringent processes and acceptance criteria: for example, at the end of the monthly or sometimes even quarterly release cycles. It became apparent to us that the only way to overcome this bottleneck would be to integrate the IT operations staff into agile teams, automating their processes to a high degree and making them part of the broader agile transformation. This marked the start of DevOps in our organisation.

Many companies stop their agile transformation at this stage because they consider agility to be "agile" as an IT method, but we wanted to go further. We realised that some other areas of the business were still holding us back and preventing us from making full use of the speed and therefore the true benefits that agile methods could offer for the company. Let me give you a few examples of what such "agility inhibitors" may look like in traditional, hierarchically organised companies. Any resemblance to actual people or organisational units in a company I may have worked for is purely coincidental and not intentional:

- The marketing department refuses to roll out the new functionalities of the mobile app because a marketing campaign to promote a range of new app functions is not due to take place for several months.
- The finance department refuses to release further funds for modifications to the application demanded by the market because

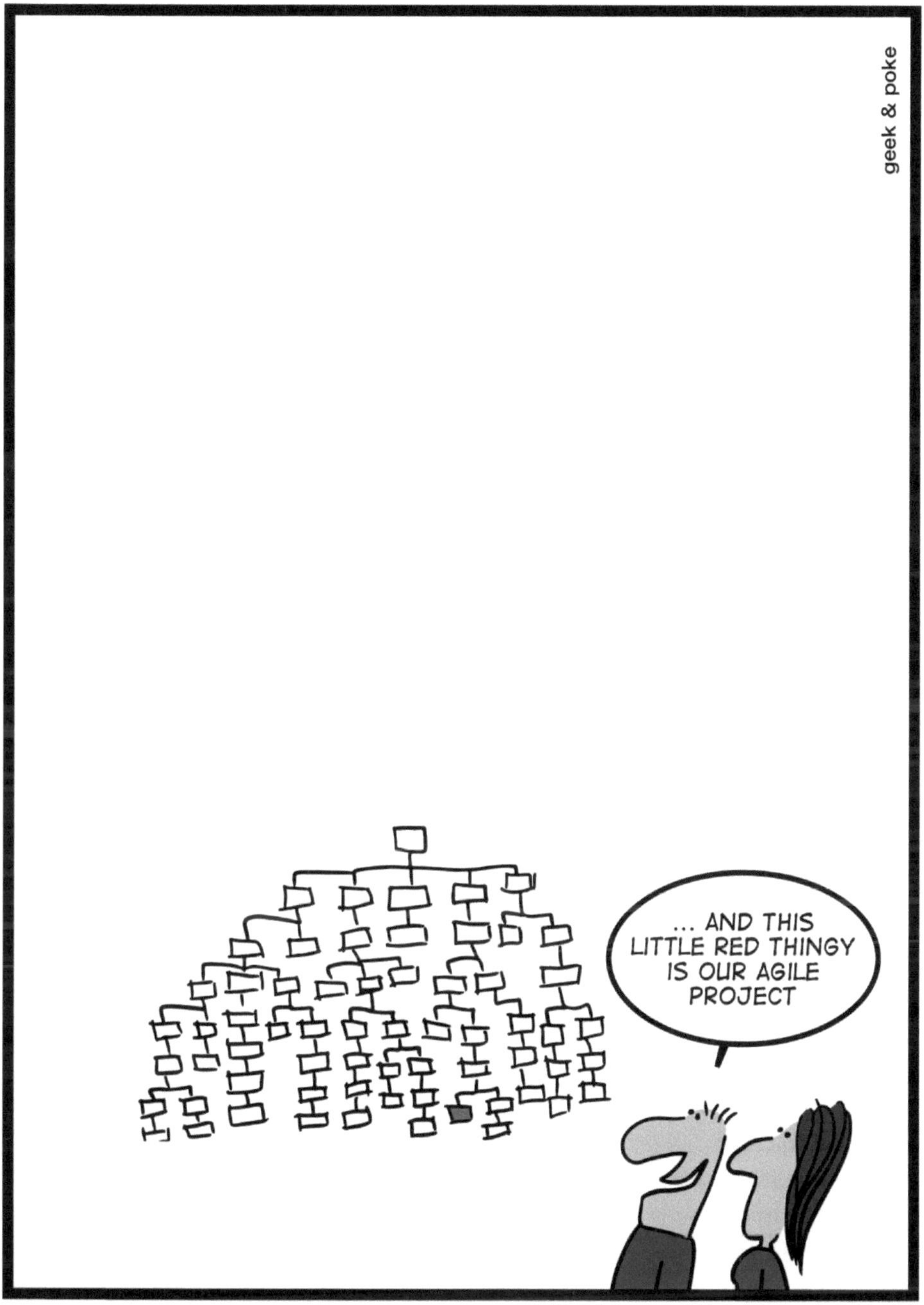

FINALLY WE'RE AGILE!

the budget for the year has already been spent and finance insists that all activities be suspended until new funds are approved as part of the next regular annual budget process.

- The HR department refuses to recognise the team with an immediate award for their outstanding work after an important, successful sprint because the annual process for awards – the company's "Chairman's Award" – nomination is already completed, and the team should therefore be nominated during next year's cycle.

I could probably go on providing examples of units and functions within traditional, hierarchical silos, but I think my point has been made clear. A company cannot restrict agility to IT if it wants to reap the full benefits from the increased speed that agile ways of working offer. True agility requires a company-wide transformation.

Many of the traditional planning and project management methods that have served us well in the past are now as outdated as hierarchical structures and their bureaucratic processes, which often serve only as an end in themselves for corporate functions and overhead structures. These traditional, hierarchical structures with their rigid planning, control, and financial processes date back to the industrial age of the last century (Taylorism) and are no longer suitable for the new agile paradigm – nor are they compatible with it.

When working on projects managed in the traditional way using waterfall methods, I observed that teams spend a lot of time waiting for other people. In many project reviews, a common answer to the question "Why is the project running behind schedule?" is "We are waiting for unit A to deliver item X". In some cases, business units may need to sign off on specifications or test cases or carry out acceptance tests, while in others it might be due to the internal bureaucracy, such as enterprise architecture needing to approve the solution architecture, cybersecurity having to sign off on the risks, or IT Operations having to provide servers (either physically, or virtually in the cloud). In other cases, external factors, such as delays by suppliers of outsourced components, may be holding up the project.

Why do we spend so much time waiting for other project stakeholders? To put it simply, because of the strict separation of duties and roles in the industrialised approach, which leads to multiple handovers and too much overhead. Ron van Kemenade[7], a former CIO colleague at ING Bank in the Netherlands, whom I greatly admire, is one of the pioneers and strong advocates of agile ways of working. A few years ago, he told me: *"Agile is primarily about avoiding handovers. Handovers slow down processes and are the source of errors."* He could not have put it better.

The novel *"The Phoenix Project"*[8] aptly demonstrates the value of focusing on simplicity – *"the art of maximising the amount of work not done"* – by removing everything unnecessary. Similar to lean methods in manufacturing, simplicity is about avoiding bottlenecks and minimising "work in progress", i.e. semi-finished products that tie up capital unnecessarily.

In his book *"The Delicate Art of Bureaucracy"*[9] Mark Schwartz beautifully describes how important it is to reduce unnecessary bureaucracy to increase agility. The way I see it, an agile approach is less about meticulously using yet another methodology (Scrum, Kanban, SAFe, Holacracy, etc.), which merely reintroduces bureaucracy in another form, but instead is about adopting a mindset that concentrates on

---

7   https://www.linkedin.com/in/ronvankemenade/

8   Kim, Gene, Kevin Behr, and George Spafford: *The Phoenix Project*. IT Revolution Press, 2018.

9   Schwartz, Marc: *The Delicate Art of Bureaucracy: Digital Transformation with the Monkey, the Razor, and the Sumo Wrestler.* IT Revolution Press, 2020.

disseminating a few principles across the entire company (not just IT). These include:

- Reducing handovers, hierarchies, and bureaucracy, and instead creating integrated and self-organising teams that can make their own decisions with very lean governance
- Embracing a positive attitude toward people, which includes extending trust in employees to get their jobs done. Getting out of the way and letting your people work. Reduction of control mechanisms, refraining from micro-management, and streamlining reporting and oversight processes
- Reducing the size of work packages and the amount of "work in progress" (semi-finished products) to shorten the cycle time
- Focusing on constant and continual improvements instead of clearly defined projects and on iterative adjustments instead of long, complicated, and highly detailed plans.

As you can see, these principles have little to do with IT specifically and can be applied across all areas of a company. As agile methods already have an established tradition in IT and experience has therefore been gained, the CIO is well positioned to drive the process of an agile transformation across the entire company. CIOs should support their business colleagues to become more agile by adopting these principles and helping them challenge assumptions and change mindsets within their organisational areas. This attitude is an important element of the role of the modern CIO, who must create added value for their company and exert a positive influence on the business. Today's CIOs are expected not merely to lead primarily inwardly within their IT organisation, but to come out of the "back office" and lead outwardly while engaging with the core business and with customers. They can do this by changing the traditional role of IT as a support unit and actively driving the agile transformation of the entire company.

Consumerisation of IT and BYOx: Control of IT procurement shifts to the users

Just a decade ago, the technology that we used at work in our companies was far more advanced than whatever most people could afford at home. Computing power, storage, and connectivity were so expensive that only companies operating at scale could afford to use them extensively. Today, the situation has reversed, and many of us now use technologies and tools at home that are more advanced and sophisticated than what companies provide in the workplace. Modern technologies are easy to use for end users, thanks to a simple "plug-and-play" approach, and the rapid adoption of constantly evolving technologies far exceeds the capabilities of traditional corporate IT. Companies often lag behind in terms of technological development, paralysed by outdated legacy systems that cannot easily be replaced. This circumstance inhibits a higher cadence in the introduction of the latest tools and technologies.

In today's workplace, employees expect the same sophisticated, user-friendly technologies that they are accustomed to at home. They also increasingly bring their own technology with them into the office. Restricting and dictating what technologies, devices, and tools employees can use in the workplace is an increasingly impossible task for CIOs. Employees, especially among the younger generation, want to use the technology and tools that allow them to work most efficiently, and they often have little regard for company standards and rules in this area. They want to bring their own technology with them to work, connect their devices, and use them to access corporate systems and information, as well as the public internet and social media simultaneously. They also want to use the apps and software packages which they are familiar with.

I remember discussing this topic with other CIOs at an event in 2014. At the time, most of them were convinced that their companies would never allow their employees to connect private devices to the company network. At Emirates, this had been standard practice for many years. I wonder whether their views have changed since then. Even back then, I was already convinced that companies, and especially CIOs, would need to rethink their policies if they wanted to be considered as modern employers who can attract the top talents from the younger generation.

Companies must open up their systems and networks to their employees – as well as to their partners – and enable them to connect their personal devices, tools, and applications. The paradigm that companies provide their employees with all the IT equipment and applications that they require for their work is antiquated and no longer fit for purpose. Members of the younger generation want to bring their own devices such as smartphones, tablets, laptops, etc. with them to the workplace, and they want to use their own applications and tools. This trend is taking off rapidly.

Just a few years ago, we talked about "bring your own device" (BYOD), and now we are faced with "bring your own technology" (BYOT) or "bring your own anything" (BYOx). This trend will continue to gain traction, especially as the IoT is continuing to expand, and all kinds of everyday objects are being equipped with sensors and getting networked. We will soon see networked glasses, networked hearing aids, smart shoes, and other IoT-enabled devices and wearables appearing in our corporate offices. It would be naïve to think that CIOs will be able to prevent these things from being connected to the corporate network. In addition, in line with the virtualisation of objects, more and more items that were used in physical form until very recently have been or are being dematerialised. These virtual objects now "live" in the cloud or on users' devices and must be able to interoperate with company systems and applications that are also increasingly stored in the cloud. Even the company network itself will probably soon be superfluous or virtualised.

At Emirates Airlines, we had already developed the concept of an "infrastructure-less office" in 2014. In this new office model, all devices (PCs, printers, etc.) were connected directly to the internet, with no local network and no local file or print servers, nor any similar hardware, because these were already in the cloud (a private cloud, in our case). At a fast-growing airline, when you add about 20 new destinations to your network each year, you have to set up at least one sales office, one airport office, and one cargo office in each destination, which adds up to a minimum of 60 new offices every year. The more quickly and easily these offices can be equipped, the better. This concept could of course also be implemented in larger locations.

Leaders will have to accept that an increasingly significant share of IT devices and software will be selected, purchased, and managed by their users and no longer by a central IT organisation under the control of the CIO. On the other hand, CIOs need to open up access to the company's IT resources – including applications, systems, and data – to enable collaboration via technologies controlled by end users, while still ensuring the security of corporate resources. Cybersecurity risks are a challenge to be managed, not a reason for sticking to an old and outdated paradigm.

Reversing the outsourcing craze: Back-sourcing, or: "How much IT should remain in-house?"

We are currently witnessing two different movements around the question of keeping technology competence within the company versus outsourcing or using IT services from a cloud supplier. Almost 20 years ago, Nicholas Carr posited in his article *"IT doesn't matter"*[10] that IT is simply a commodity with no strategic value for companies and that a third-party provider specialising in IT services (including software development) could provide that commodity more cheaply and effectively than in-house IT professionals. He believed that the only relevant concerns for IT were the cost and quality of the service provided. Since IT was not seen as strategic, a dedicated external supplier would be best placed to provide these services. He therefore encouraged companies to outsource IT as a competitively neutral component in order to save costs of their operations.

In the past two decades, however, the situation has changed significantly. Digitalisation has become a strategic topic, and companies have been confronted with the fact that technology increasingly defines their future, and therefore IT has become an important strategic component. Many companies that jumped on the outsourcing bandwagon are now realising, often painfully, that they went too far, outsourcing too much of their technological competence to third parties and not retaining sufficient IT knowledge and skills in-house. As a result, they now lack

---

10   https://hbr.org/2003/05/it-doesnt-matter

much-needed technical competencies and are far too dependent on their IT and software-development suppliers. Consequently, many companies are now working hard to rebuild their in-house IT competences – a process known as in-sourcing or back-sourcing – because this supposed "commodity" has become a strategic core element of their business.

This is one side of the story. On the other side, an increasing number of services can now simply be consumed as cloud services, making a significant part of the physical IT infrastructure and in-house software development redundant. It has become very easy for a start-up to source and combine all kinds of services from the cloud very quickly, without any major investment, and without ever having to own a physical server or write a single line of code. Just two decades ago, this was completely unthinkable.

The question of whether to own or outsource data centres and other IT hardware is almost obsolete. For most services and applications, it has even become irrelevant, as the services can simply be consumed from the cloud. The traditional horizontal layering of technology stacks (hardware, storage, operating systems, middleware, applications, etc.) has largely been replaced by fully integrated vertical services. In this model, the underlying technology is effectively invisible and largely irrelevant to the consumer of the services. A company that uses Salesforce, ServiceNow, or WorkDay leaves the entire technology stack to the provider of these cloud services and has no real interest in what hardware or operating system the application is running on. However, these cloud services mostly address standardised and non-competitive support functions and contribute to hardly any strategic processes in the company's value chain. To fully exploit the technical possibilities of such services, it is still necessary to understand the various underlying technologies.

Software has become an essential part of services and products and hence one of the most strategic components of any company. Due to dematerialisation, an ever-growing number of products and services are becoming "software-defined". This once again raises the question of whether to "make or buy" software, which is increasingly coming back to the table and into the centre of strategic decisions. If software is becoming an essential component of products and services and is therefore a strategic differentiator in the market and a source of competitive advantage, companies will want to ensure that they have this expertise in-house. No one wants to outsource to a third-party company the development of and control over strategic components that could offer a competitive advantage. Another question now arises, which is where to draw the boundaries between strategic components and "commodities". I believe that there is no definite answer to this question. However, experience has shown that many supposedly competition-neutral "commodities" can in fact contribute to the creation of a competitive advantage.

One frequently cited example is Tesla. As discussed in previous chapters, Tesla sees itself more as a software company than as a car manufacturer. A large share of a Tesla vehicle's functionality is defined and controlled by software. A new Tesla model is often "just" a software upgrade. Customers can purchase new functions or improvements online simply by downloading a software upgrade and installing it in their vehicle, "over-the-air". Tesla's decision to develop its own ERP system and therefore build a large part of its IT in-house was based on strategic reasons and had nothing to do with cost optimisation à la Nicholas Carr. Companies like Tesla have recognised that IT is strategic, and to use technology effectively as a strategic asset they will increasingly bring IT expertise back in-house. Benefits such as agility and shorter time-to-market cycles, product innovation, and personalised service offerings for customers can be achieved only with great difficulty if most IT functions are outsourced to third parties and developments must be planned for years to come and coordinated with the supplier well in advance. A "90-day forecast" is often the best that can be expected, and such processes are simply not compatible with the agile approach required to accelerate time-to-market cycles and to stay ahead of the competition.

Modern-day leaders will need to carefully rethink the strategic value of IT before blindly following the cost-driven outsourcing path. They will also need to ensure that they have the necessary in-house techno-logical expertise and capabilities to drive the strategic digital agenda within their companies.

13

Technology as a topic for the board of directors

Only a decade ago, most companies saw IT as a necessary evil, an annoying cost factor. This perspective was also implicit in the Nicholas Carr article *"IT doesn't matter"*, which I mentioned in the previous chapter. However, the digitalisation wave of the last decade has made it clear to most companies that IT is much more than just a competition-neutral commodity or a simple business support tool. IT has long since become an important strategic asset that will determine the future of almost every company while driving a large share of all innovation. Technology – and IT in particular – has long since become a strategic core component of practically every company.

As IT today is a key strategic factor, one would also expect it to be reflected in the make-up of companies' boards of directors, including non-executive boards or supervisory boards. Despite IT's strategic nature, however, very few companies have made IT and digitalisation a topic worth establishing and discussing on an ongoing basis at the board of directors' level. Outside of the technology sector, few larger companies have appointed people to their boards of directors who can bring an in-depth knowledge of IT and experience with digitalisation or digital transformation to the company's top strategic body. I am not talking about token appointments in which someone from the local national office of large technology companies such as Google, HPE, IBM, or Microsoft is appointed to the board of directors to keep up appearances. These local offices are primarily sales entities, and their managers are certainly good salespeople and networkers, but they generally have little or no direct experience with large-scale digital transformation because major initiatives of this type are designed and implemented by corporate head offices or in the production facilities, rather than at the level of a national sales organisation. According to Constellation Research,[11] a leading technology research and consulting firm in Silicon Valley, in 2019 "only approximately 11% of Fortune-500 companies had experienced tech experts on their boards of directors".

In the future, technology will determine how products and services are designed, developed, produced, and marketed; how companies inter-act with their customers, suppliers, and partners; and how they collab-orate internally. Companies that want to be successful in this digital and networked economy will therefore need to have people on their board of directors with experience in technology and especially with digital transformation. Boards of directors must understand how dig-ital transformation can change their business models, products, and services and how the company can be structured to work efficiently in the digital age. They need members who have practical experience driving the digital agenda and can comprehend its impact on the cul-ture, processes, and organisational structure of established companies — not people who have read a book on the subject or consultants who advise companies on "how things should be done" in areas where they have no direct experience themselves.

A 2019 study published in the *Sloan Management Review* entitled *"It Pays to Have a Digitally Savvy Board"*[12] showed that boards whose mem-bers understand the impact of new technologies on business success help companies to outperform the competition. The study found that *"being a digitally savvy director is often a consequence of time spent in a high-clock-speed industry where business models change quickly, such*

---

11   https://www.constellationr.com/

12   https://sloanreview.mit.edu/article/it-pays-to-have-a-digitally-savvy-board /#:~:text=When%20a%20board%20lacks%20digital,company%20to%20a%20 successful%20future

as software or telecom, or having experience in an executive role with a strong technology component".

If one looks at the composition of the boards of directors of most established companies, one finds that they are still overwhelmingly made up of sales, finance, and legal experts, as well as people with in-depth experience of the company's traditional core business, i.e., people who know how the business has been run successfully in the past. If these companies want to ensure that they also remain relevant and competitive in the future, they must change fundamentally. If they fail to use IT as a strategic advantage, to digitalise their business processes and products and exploit new technology-driven business models and distribution channels, these companies run the risk of becoming marginalised. *"Digital Darwinism is unkind to those who wait,"* says Ray Wang, founder and CEO of Constellation Research, and this conclusion is also underpinned by the numbers. For example, *Forbes*[13] recently observed that more than half of all companies that were on the Fortune 500 list in the year 2000 are no longer on it. They have been acquired, gone bankrupt, shrunk into irrelevance, or disappeared completely – in most cases because they failed to leverage technology to strategically realign or reinvent their business.

Having more IT and digital transformation experts on the board of directors will also help shift the strategic discussion on the board towards technology. IT is becoming a central strategic topic. CIOs must become more involved and gain greater visibility with the board of directors to ensure that the topic of technology is on the agenda. They must also think more strategically and determine how best to communicate at the board level to contribute to the strategic agenda of the company.

---

13   https://www.forbes.com/sites/oracle/2014/12/19/ray-wang-cloud-is-the-foundation-for-digital-transformation/

For entrepreneurial-minded CIOs with experience in digital transformation, this approach can create new career opportunities, such as assuming a role as non-executive director on a board of directors. In addition, joining a board of directors can be a good opportunity for any CIO to develop, learn, and begin acquiring the necessary strategic skills to drive transformation across their company.

Networks instead of hierarchies

When I was in high school, I learnt programming in BASIC on an HP 9800 series computer, a desktop computer with a 32-character LED display. In 1980, Sharp launched the PC-1211, the first pocket computer, which was actually a calculator that could be programmed in BASIC. I bought this wonderful device with the pocket money I had earned working as an usher in the evenings at the local cinema in the small town where my family lived.

A year later, the Sinclair ZX81 hit the market. This was one of the first home computers with a membrane keyboard that could be connected to a television as a display via a coaxial antenna cable. It came with 1 KB of random-access memory (RAM), and an expansion module with 16 KB of RAM (56 KB usable) could be purchased separately. As I could not afford this investment at the time, I looked around for another opportunity to earn some money, and so, on school-free afternoons, I stocked shelves at the local discount shop to earn some extra income until, about a year later, I was able to buy a second-hand Sinclair ZX81 as my first home computer. As we had only a simple black-and-white TV set at home at the time, connecting it to my Sinclair ZX81 was a frequent source of conflict with my father, who wanted to watch the news. My next purchase was an Atari 800, for which I then bought my own small second-hand colour TV as a display screen. To afford this investment, I worked on a construction site at a steel construction company for several weeks during the school breaks. As a result, I spent a large part of my youth at home on the computer, which influenced my studies and ultimately my choice of career.

Because it takes time to rise through the ranks of hierarchical organisations, most current CIOs and other C-suite executives of larger companies are likely between 45 and 65 years old, which means they belong to my generation. These CIOs were born in the 1960s or 1970s. Most of them went to school primarily in the 1970s and 1980s, were taught by teachers who were probably born in the 1940s, and used course materials from the 1950s. Our school years have an immense impact on our views, beliefs, and values, and they shape us for the rest of our lives. These CIOs went to school in the last millennium, when education was heavily influenced by the methods and beliefs of the industrial age and when computers were primarily used as mainframes in larger companies. Back then, computers were hardly used in private life and were mainly of interest to computer geeks, like I was at the time.

During the industrial age, the predominant form of organisation was the hierarchical structure, adopted from the military, wherein the basic principle was to separate the "thinking" from the "doing". The individual tasks assigned to workers were distinct from one another and structured in such a way that each worker knew precisely what they were expected to do and how their performance would be measured. Information was shared on a need-to-know basis, which meant that most employees knew very little about what was going on in other parts of the company. Workers on the production line were not supposed to worry about what was happening upstream or downstream of them. They were supposed to concentrate on their work and do it as efficiently as possible, and thinking about other parts of the company was regarded as a distraction. Managers kept information to themselves, because knowledge equalled power. The higher one rose in the company, the more information became available, but it always had to be kept secret. This was one of the major principles of Taylorism, with its focus on the separation of duties, extreme specialisation, and measurability. Essentially, hierarchical structures were introduced to separate people from one another. Most of today's C-suite executives had an education

106

dominated by the paradigms of the industrial age, and their early work experience was infused with Taylorism, which was at the time generally accepted as a framework for how companies should be run. Naturally, they were conditioned by the assumptions and doctrines that prevailed at the time.

The younger generation is growing up in the digital age, however, where other principles predominate and other rules apply. A couple of years ago, as I watched my daughter doing her homework, I realised how completely different things are today compared to when I was at school in the 1970s and 1980s. Back then, we did our homework ourselves, kept it to ourselves, and hid it from each other because we wanted to outperform our classmates. The environment was very competitive, and the dominant paradigm was: "The more I know and keep to myself, the better I will perform relative to my classmates". In other words, "knowledge is power".

When my daughter was still at school and doing her homework, she would work on a topic, prepare her first draft – in other words, a minimal viable product (MVP) – and share it on WhatsApp or another social media tool that she and her classmates used to communicate with each other. Within a few hours, many of her classmates had expanded and improved the MVP through multiple iterations and continued to share it onward using these social media tools until the output achieved a level of maturity and quality that none of the students could have produced on their own in such a short time. In effect, the younger generation crowd-source their homework, an approach that did not exist when I was at school. This generation is growing up in a world characterised by the sharing economy, crowd-sourcing, and crowd-funding, by Wikipedia, open-source software, freeware, and much more. The mindset in this world is: "The more I share, the more my entire network benefits, and hence so do I". They know that no one person is smarter than a network of people working together efficiently. They intuitively understand the power of networks. Many managers who believe that they are demi-gods and think that they know everything better should mull over this sentence: "No one person is smarter than a network of people!" What a powerful approach, and so different from the "knowledge is power" paradigm that I and probably most of us grew up with.

The paradigm and mindset that prevail in large companies reflect the fact that most C-suite executives were educated in the industrial age, but digital transformation is about exploring new technology-driven business models, and it therefore breaks through the well-established, rigid, hierarchical organisational silos that still dominate most large companies today. In my opinion, this is one of the main reasons that digital transformation initiatives fail so often: managers at the top of the company want to preserve the power and influence that they have painstakingly accrued and solidified over years within their individual silos. It is still mostly the case that importance within a company relates directly to the number of people one manages and the size of the budget one controls – that is, to one's direct managerial responsibility within a hierarchical silo. Corporate titles and job-grade concepts (e.g., from Hay) are still based on this strictly hierarchical concept, and titles continue to matter more than the content and quality of one's work. This strict title hierarchy is still widespread and dominant today, especially in the Anglo-Saxon world. When I ask someone from the United States what they do for a living, I often receive the answer: "I'm a Vice President".

In his book *"Rich Dad Poor Dad"*[14], Robert Kiyosaki recalls how his "rich dad" (actually the father of his best friend, who was a very successful entrepreneur) described the difference between an entrepreneur and

---

14   Kiyosaki, Robert: *Rich Dad Poor Dad: What the Rich Teach Their Kids About Money That the Poor and Middle Class Do Not!* Plata Publishing, 2017.

an employee. I won't cite the exact wording, but the meaning went as follows:

Entrepreneurs have an incentive to spend as little of the company's money as possible to maximise their returns and ensure the company's financial sustainability. Employees, on the other hand, have an incentive to spend as much money as possible, because the more people they manage and the greater the budget they control (and spend), the more important they are in the company.

These incentives are even stronger when job security or bonuses and other rewards are tied to a manager's budget size or "span of control" (i.e., the number of employees for whom the manager is directly responsible). For example, employees may request larger budgets to justify their role or increase the number of employees under their purview even when doing so is not in the company's best interest.

The digitalisation and the virtualisation of physical products within current business models and processes is already breaking through organisational silos and challenging many established roles, functions, jobs, and corporate units. Our highly networked world in the digital age calls for a different way of structuring and organising companies and new rules of collaboration. It is not primarily the hierarchical position and title, the reporting lines, the size of the budget, or the number of employees managed that are important, but the added value that a leader brings to the company and the positive impact that they can achieve regardless of who is responsible for the resources involved. The relevant thing here is not individual goals, but rather the overall contribution to the company's purpose and objectives, which are not always purely financial in nature but increasingly comprise a combined "triple bottom line" consisting of the company's financial, social, and environmental contributions.

If companies want to be successful in the digital age, they must become networks themselves and move away from purely hierarchical structures, as Peter Hinssen describes in his superb best-seller, *"The Network Always Wins"*.[15] If they want to attract and retain talent from the younger generation, they must offer their employees a purpose, an environment, and a corporate culture that match their values and with which they can identify themselves. The sharing paradigm of networks is better suited to this mission than the hierarchical structures and paradigms of Taylorism from the industrial age.

However, most companies cannot do away with hierarchies entirely. Only very small companies and some start-ups can manage without any hierarchy whatsoever. A few larger companies have attempted to completely eliminate hierarchy, but these experiments often ended in chaos and had to be reversed. Even more modern forms of organisation, such as Holacracy,[16] include a certain degree of hierarchy, but more in relation to the skills of the employees than to their job title or status. There are countless books on the topic of non-hierarchical organisation, but some of these forms are very restrictive in my opinion. Others, such as Holacracy, in their pure form suggest a relatively large administrative overhead, which can once again escalate into bureaucracy. Certain concepts can be adjusted and combined, however, as described in *"Reinventing Organizations"*[17] by Frederic Laloux, *"Unboss"*[18] by Jacob Bøtter and Lars Kolind, or *"Humanocracy"*[19] by Gary Hamel and Michele Zanini.

---

15   https://www.peterhinssen.com/books/the-network-always-wins

16   Holacracy is a decentralised management system developed by Ternary Software founder Brian Robertson. See: https://www.holacracy.org/

17   https://www.reinventingorganizations.com/

18   Bøtter, Jacob/Kolind, Lars: *Unboss.* Jyllands-Postens Forlag, 2012.

19   Hamel, Gary/Zanini, Michele: *Humanocracy: Creating Organizations as Amazing as the People Inside Them.* Harvard Business Review Press, 2020.

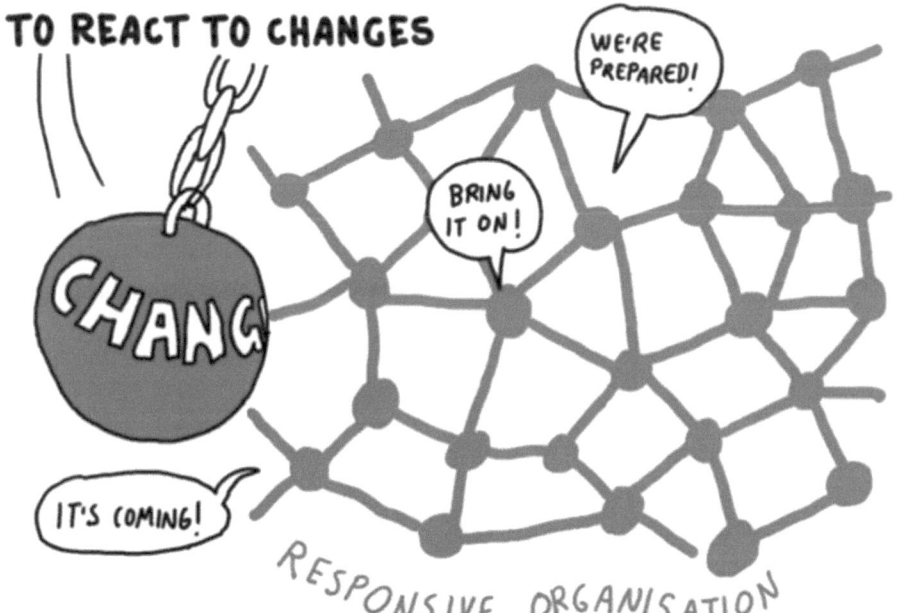

Most companies have a long and deeply rooted tradition of hierarchical structures. This tradition is part of the company's DNA. It cannot simply be tossed aside from one day to another, and it need not be. As Peter Hinssen puts it in *"The Network Always Wins"*, hierarchies and network structures can coexist perfectly well. This assertion may sound a little strange at first, because the two forms of organisation can appear incompatible or contradictory. Being averse to ambiguity, one assumes that there can be either a hierarchy or a network, but not both. In organisational theory, however, it must also be possible to combine contradictory concepts – hierarchy AND network, not hierarchy OR network. I call this organisational form, which combines hierarchy and network, the "quantum organisation".

As shown in the previous chapter, technological competencies are increasingly distributed across various units within a company and are no longer concentrated in a centralised IT department. CIOs are well placed to lead the development of a new organisational paradigm for their companies based on well-established methods and the ways of working in IT. These include the use of interdisciplinary teams in agile structures, DevOps, iterative product development, crowd sourcing, and collaboration with open-source communities. Disseminating these approaches across the firm represents a major opportunity for CIOs to support their companies as they transition to the digital age.

Quantum organisation: A new organisational paradigm for the network age

What is a quantum organisation? Both the name and the underlying principle derive from physics. In the 17th century, a controversy erupted among physicists regarding the nature of light: did it consist of particles, or was it an energy wave? In some circumstances, light appeared to have the properties of particles, but in others it behaved like a wave. These two apparently contradictory characteristics of light could not be explained and reconciled in a combined theory until 1913, when Niels Bohr[20], one of the greatest physicists and thinkers of the 20th century, presented a combined model in which electromagnetic radiation (light is a form of electromagnetic radiation) could be described both as particles and as waves. This marked the birth of quantum physics. In quantum physics, the physical features of light are described in a duality[21] of waves and particles. Light can behave differently depending on the context or even depending on the observer, who influences the behaviour of light by observing it. The concept of the quantum organisation is deeply rooted in physics, and I am convinced that we can learn many lessons from physics (i.e., from the study of nature) that will help resolve other seemingly complex or unsolvable contradictions in organisational development and in other fields.

As described in earlier chapters, the business world is no longer linear, as it was during the industrial era, but is now overwhelmingly dominated by networks. For companies in this networked economy to

---

20   https://en.wikipedia.org/wiki/Niels_Bohr

21   https://en.wikipedia.org/wiki/Wave%E2%80%93particle_duality

be successful and survive, appropriate organisational models are required. Traditional hierarchical models from the industrial age are no longer necessarily the best way to organise a company, as they are ill equipped to cope with the complexity of a networked environment.

In physics, the classical Newtonian laws no longer apply once one enters the subatomic world and observes objects with a very high speed (approaching the speed of light) or subject to extreme gravitational forces. Similarly, the classical industrial approach to structuring and organising a company no longer works effectively in the network age. With quantum mechanics, which replaced Newton's laws in the subatomic realm, and the theory of relativity, which replaced them in the 'very large' and 'very fast' realms, physicists in the early 20th century had to adopt completely new paradigms and essentially throw the foundations of classical physics overboard.

The basic principles of quantum mechanics were described in the *"Copenhagen Interpretation"*[22], which was largely developed by Niels Bohr and Werner Heisenberg between 1925 and 1927. According to the Copenhagen Interpretation, physical systems generally have no fixed properties prior to being measured, and quantum mechanics can predict only the probability that measurements will provide certain results. The act of measuring influences the system and causes the set of probabilities to be reduced to only one of the possible values, which is called a wave-function collapse. The inner workings of atomic and subatomic processes are necessarily not directly observable, as the act of observing would greatly affect them. While elementary particles exhibit predictable properties in some experiments, they are entirely unpredictable in others, such as attempts to identify individual particle trajectories through a simple physical apparatus.

---

22   https://en.wikipedia.org/wiki/Copenhagen_interpretation#:~:text=Copenhagen
%2Dtype%20interpretations%20hold%20that,and%20other%20arbitrary%20
mental%20factors

Classical physics draws a distinction between particles and waves. It also relies on continuity and determinism in natural phenomena. In the early 20th century, newly discovered atomic and subatomic phenomena appeared to defy these principles. Quantum mechanics cannot easily be reconciled with everyday language and observation. Quantum interpretations often appear counterintuitive, even to the physicists who develop them. The properties of the system are subject to a principle of incompatibility. Certain properties cannot be defined jointly for the same system at the same time. This incompatibility is expressed quantitatively through Heisenberg's uncertainty principle. For example, if a particle has a fixed location at a certain point in time, it is meaningless to talk about its momentum at that instant. This also means that the precise properties of a subatomic particle cannot be determined absolutely but are always dependent on the observer and the context. The very moment that an attempt is made to measure the properties of the particle (e.g., an electron), the observer interacts with the observed object and thereby changes its behaviour. This means that the exact position of a particle is always relative to the observer and to its context.

The Copenhagen Interpretation is intended to indicate the proper ways of thinking and speaking about the physical meaning of the mathematical formulations of quantum mechanics and the corresponding experimental results. This approach offers due respect to discontinuity, probability, and the concept of wave-particle duality. In some respects, it denies standard causality. The wave-particle duality describes the dual nature of subatomic particles that sometimes act as fixed objects and sometimes as energy waves. An experiment can show particle-like properties or wave-like properties according to Bohr's complementarity principle.

Two camps of scientists fought for centuries over what they both believed to be the "only truth". One camp was convinced that light was a particle, while the other had evidence that it had to be waves. The fact that both sides had experimental evidence that served as "evidence" for their theories kept the conflict alive. Only with the arrival of quantum mechanics did the "schizophrenic" character of light begin to make sense and today the scientific world agrees that light, as well as other subatomic particles, can behave both as particles and as waves simultaneously.

Another organisational principle that can be derived from physics relates to the observation that the properties of a particle (e.g., its mass, charge, position, speed) manifest themselves only when the particle interacts with other particles. A single particle on its own has no measurable properties. In his book on quantum electrodynamics, *"QED: The Strange Theory of Light and Matter"*[23], the great physicist Richard Feynman[24] describes how subatomic particles interact with one another by exchanging even smaller particles such as photons and other forms of energy (e.g., gluons, W particles). The nature and essence of particles are mainly determined by these energy exchanges and are not primarily properties of their own. This means that only the interactions between particles are essential and thus define the properties of the particles themselves.

A further property of particles, one rooted in Albert Einstein's[25] special theory of relativity[26], is that matter is only a manifestation of energy. Einstein's most famous equation, $E = mc^2$, underpins this mathematically. In advanced experimental physics, scientists attempt to find ever-smaller subatomic particles that make up the universe (e.g., quarks, leptons, bosons). Experiments using the Large Hadron Collider (LHC)

---

23   https://en.wikipedia.org/wiki/QED:_The_Strange_Theory_of_Light_and_Matter

24   https://en.wikipedia.org/wiki/Richard_Feynman

25   https://en.wikipedia.org/wiki/Albert_Einstein

26   https://en.wikipedia.org/wiki/Special_relativity

at the European Organisation for Nuclear Research (CERN) near Geneva have revealed a strange phenomenon: when scientists used extremely high energy to "shoot" subatomic particles at each other, in order to split them into even smaller particles, they observed that the newly created particle fragments could have a larger mass than the original particles. This can be explained by the fact that energy can be converted into matter and vice-versa. The extremely high energy used to break the particles into smaller components was converted into matter and created larger particles instead of the smaller ones that were expected. It is not difficult to imagine how this could be repeated indefinitely, and scientists will therefore be busy for a long time breaking particles into smaller components in their attempts to find the "ultimate" smallest components or building blocks of the universe. This again means that the particles themselves are not really relevant, but only the interactions between them, namely the exchange of energy, which can also be seen in the three basic concepts of quantum physics:

1. A particle cannot be assigned an exact and unique trajectory (position and speed) in space, but only a probability, depending on its context and the observer.
2. The properties of a particle itself are not primarily relevant but are solely defined by the interactions between particles.
3. Subatomic phenomena can appear both as waves and as particles depending on the observer.

Once we understand that nature is not linear, but dominated by networks, it becomes clear that we should look closely at these subatomic structures and interactions as we attempt to develop organisations that can thrive in a networked economy. If we apply these principles to organisations, we can derive insights into how they function and attempt to formulate a new organisational paradigm for the network age:

117

- Individuals, resources, and teams should not be assigned to a definite position (unit, job, role, level, or reporting line) within the organisation but should always have a certain probability (fuzziness) of being in a certain position depending on the context, situation, and observer.
- Organisational structures and positions are not relevant in themselves but are a manifestation of the interactions between the "actors" (individuals, resources, and teams), both within and outside the organisation, and thus the relationships between them matter more than their organisational affiliations.
- While networks dominate, hierarchy *and* network can exist simultaneously, and much like the wave-particle duality, the observed characteristics of the organisation depend on the context and observer. We will have to live with the "schizophrenic" character of organisations, just as physicists had to accept wave-particle duality.

I have not yet been able to describe what exactly a quantum organisational model would look like or how it would be implemented, but the abovementioned analogy from physics provides a basic outline. I believe that agile IT organisations are close to developing a fully realised quantum organisation and that these concepts and principles can be extended to other areas of a company.

16

Data

Data is, of course, a crucial element in digitalisation and a key factor in the evolving role of IT and the CIO. The proper management of data in a company is essential, and while "data-driven" is yet another buzzword, it does speak to a real need for high-quality quantifiable information. However, companies should be data-driven only within the context of the criteria described in the previous chapter and not merely for the sake of it.

Although much has been written about the role of data in the corporation, I believe that several key aspects of data are often neglected. One of these is timeliness. Analytical methods are often applied to outdated data, which leads to suboptimal results. Just a few short seconds can make data outdated, even worthless. In a stock exchange, milliseconds can mean a difference of millions of dollars in the value of share packages. Similarly, in the airline industry, the price of a seat is calculated in real time based on the remaining inventory, market demand, and other factors such as the expected booking behaviour of customers. In the thousands of transactions per second that the reservation system of a large airline needs to process, the number of seats still available – and hence their price – is often determined in milliseconds. This form of data-driven price optimisation in the airline industry, known as "revenue management", often determines whether an airline is profitable or not. Relying on outdated data would be fatal.

I have learnt from experience to always make all data available in real time. No outdated "batch mode", where data is copied over once an hour, nor any caching. In operational environments, the value of data decreases exponentially over time, so everything must be in real time. This kind of timeliness is by no means guaranteed, even in the high-pressure environment of a stock exchange. I am always amazed when I read a newspaper and find that it still prints pages of stock prices from the previous day. Who on earth is interested in this outdated, largely worthless data? In the digital world, day-old stock data is less valuable than the paper on which it is printed.

Old data can be useful in the aggregate, however. Changes and trends are often significantly more valuable than absolute numbers. When the news reports that the Dow Jones Index closed at 39,497.54 points or that the euro-to-dollar exchange rate is 0.92 EUR/USD, what does that mean for us? Is it good or bad? Is this better or worse than the day before? Or a week ago? Or a month? When a company reports an annual profit of 2.3 billion or the construction of a railway tunnel costs 4.5 billion, is that a little or a lot? What figures are there to compare these to? Absolute figures say very little. You always have to look at them in context, review them against comparable figures, examine changes over time, and derive and recognise trends. Absolute figures often lead us astray if we do not question them and put them in the right context. Hans Rosling touches very aptly on this topic in his book, *"Factfulness"*[27]: "Our brains seduce us into a dramatising view of the world that by no means corresponds to reality".

The saying that "data is the new oil" has been common for some time. It is generally attributed to the mathematician Clive Humby[28]: *"Data is the new oil. Like oil, data is valuable, but if unrefined it cannot really be utilised. Oil has to be converted into gas, plastic, chemicals, etc., to create a valuable entity that drives profitable activity."* The commonly accepted view is that data is the new oil because new and valuable insights can be derived from it. Depending on what a company does, these insights can contribute to customer retention, upselling, new revenue models, better advertising, etc. However, I believe that this analogy between

---

27   Rosling, Hans et al.: *Factfulness: Ten reasons we're wrong about the world – and why things are better than you think.* Sceptre, 2018.

28   https://en.wikipedia.org/wiki/Clive_Humby

data and oil is flawed and can lead to inaccurate conclusions. While data is obviously valuable, it differs from oil in several crucial ways:

- Oil is valuable because it is a scarce resource available in limited quantities around the world. The same applies to gold, etc. This assessment does not apply to data, however, which is available in seemingly infinite quantities and can be copied at a negligible cost.
- Oil is a store of value, but data is not. The oil price fluctuates with demand, but in general it rises over time. Oil can be hoarded. It can be stored in barrels and will still have a value in ten years' time. Data, however, has value only if you can do something with it, apply it, and draw conclusions that lead to actions. Data loses its value exponentially over time, as we have seen above.
- Oil is consumed through use, but data is not. Indeed, data tends to increase in value the more it is used, particularly when it is combined with other data.
- Oil is what economists call a "rival good", which means the possession of oil by one person leaves less oil for everyone else. Data, by contrast, can be replicated and shared without ever being diminished. In fact, the more you share it and combine it with data from other people, the more valuable it becomes.

Failing to understand this last point often leads to an inefficient, self-defeating attitude towards data. Because it is considered valuable, people are reluctant to share it, even when doing so would make it more valuable. The more it is used, disclosed, published, shared, and combined with data from other sources, the richer the conclusions that can be drawn from it, and hence the more valuable it becomes. The "knowledge is power" paradigm that many of us inherited from the industrial age, as described in an earlier chapter, coupled with flawed comparisons to oil or other rival goods, results in the hoarding of data that should instead be disseminated. Leaders should keep this in mind when designing data strategies for their companies.

Technologies

New technologies always tend to elicit a great deal of interest, and advances in AI are perhaps the most talked-about technological development in recent years. I might well have been among the first people to see AI as an important and promising technology, having been closely involved with it already during my studies at ETH Zürich. My master's thesis at the Institute for Computer Vision in 1989 involved programming an intelligent control system for an autonomous robot vehicle on a LISP machine from Symbolics – a computer system that was at that time specifically designed for such "expert systems" but which no longer exists today. This control system was implemented as an expert system in which a simplified neural network was used to combine uncertain data from various sources, which had been analysed and assigned a probability factor. The algorithm was based on a mathematical model that utilised the Dempster-Shafer[29] theory for combining different probabilities to form a single body of evidence. Under this approach, information from different sources is combined into an overall statement using the so-called "Dempster rule of combination", which considers the credibility of the sources when calculating the combined probability. In my work, the data sources were a combination of distinct objects extracted from a camera feed on the robot vehicle and map data of the terrain over which the robot travelled. This data was estimated with a probability factor and combined, in line with the theory, to generate a statement about the positioning of the robot vehicle. At the time, there were no GPS systems in cars, no smartphones, and no camera drones.

Then came the "AI winter", and for a long time there was relatively little progress or investment in AI research, presumably because the results

---

29   https://en.wikipedia.org/wiki/Dempster%E2%80%93Shafer_theory

achieved by relatively simple applications had failed to meet expectations. At this point, algorithms were programmed, meaning a developer had to give each algorithm a sequence of specific instructions to complete defined tasks. In a chess programme, for example, a human would programme the play strategy (e.g., the approach of a grandmaster) into the algorithm, typically using "if-then-else" rules.

A huge breakthrough came in the late 2010s, when AI instances were no longer programmed but trained using deep learning and reinforced learning methods. On the 5th of December 2017, DeepMind, an artificial intelligence research institution and subsidiary of Alphabet Inc. (the parent company of Google), released a preprint of a paper introducing the AlphaZero programme. The preprint described how AlphaZero achieved superior playing strength within 24 hours through reinforced learning, beating the best-performing programmes, Stockfish, Elmo, and the three-day version of AlphaGo Zero, in their respective disciplines. AlphaZero beat the free chess programme Stockfish 8 after nine hours of self-learning.

Classic chess programmes such as Stockfish evaluate positions and pieces based on properties that are mostly defined and weighted by human grandmasters, which are combined with a high-performance alpha-beta search that generates and evaluates a huge search tree with a large number of heuristics and domain-specific adjustments. By contrast, AlphaZero's algorithm plays against itself based solely on the rules of the game. Starting with random moves, it evaluates the results and optimises its strategies by adjusting the weightings of its network. AlphaZero therefore learns exclusively based on the rules of the game and by playing millions of games against itself, without a human having to programme various game strategies. Human grandmasters who played against AlphaZero were often amazed by its unorthodox moves and by the ingenuity of the strategies it used, many of which had never been seen before. This example illustrates the potential of artificial intelligence for very specific tasks with clearly defined rules. In these situations, AI can achieve "superhuman" abilities through training, but only for very specific tasks.

At Emirates Airlines, we experimented very early on with AI. We set up our own IBM Watson instance for aviation medicine and applied machine-learning systems that could combine a wide range of different data sources for price optimisation and revenue management. Furthermore, we used AI to optimise fleet utilisation and crew rostering, introduced AI-based chatbots in call centres, and much more. Much of this technology was rolled out operationally, and it contributed significantly to the competitive advantage of Emirates Airlines and to the optimisation of costs and revenue. AI will substantially alter both corporate operations and our daily lives, and CIOs must keep pace with the latest developments in this rapidly evolving field. However, most firms do not need to hire a Chief AI Officer, just as they do not need a CDO. At the moment, there is plenty of hype about generative AI, agentic AI and large language models (LLMs). While I am convinced that this surge of interest will level off, AI will, I believe, remain a major technology topic for the foreseeable future.

Blockchain experienced a similar hype moment in the spotlight, and while that time is past, the technology remains highly relevant to a wide range of fields. Blockchain involves much more than just cryptocurrencies, and I even believe that the technology's potential remains seriously underestimated. Distributed ledger technology (DLT) offers enormous potential and can greatly simplify inter-company transactions, especially in the financial sector, by eliminating the need for an intermediary, which is currently still required to ensure credibility and security of transactions. However, too many of these intermediaries are making a fortune, and the immensely powerful global banking system currently has little appetite to simplify these processes with blockchain when doing so would undermine its own reason for being.

Technology trends are regularly hyped by the media, analysts, and consulting firms, so every executive feels pressurised to show that they are engaging with the latest innovations. Many of these technologies have gone quiet again, but that does not mean that they have vanished or become irrelevant. The hype surrounding RFID, beacons, VR/AR, the metaverse, etc. has calmed down – and this is not necessarily a bad thing – but most of these technologies continue to exist and many play important roles in corporate operations. However, the next wave of hype is already pre-programmed and will certainly occur, likely when quantum computers cross the threshold of commercial viability.

Similarly, entertainment technologies and other household electronics are especially susceptible to the hype cycle. How many people still have a curved TV in their living room or watch films at home with 3D glasses? These are technologies which, only a few years ago, we were made to believe that we absolutely needed to have and that they would become universal, but which have since largely fallen by the wayside.

Of course, I am firmly convinced that a modern CIO must always remain abreast of the latest technologies and should understand the topics being worked on in the research laboratories of the tech giants and start-ups. A CIO must also have the necessary curiosity to constantly learn and experience new things. Above all, a CIO must be able to properly identify technologies that can generate substantial added value for their company and distinguish those technologies from the noise of technologies that are merely a marketing gimmick or an over-hyped trend. Accomplishing this challenging task requires properly understanding the technologies themselves. My advice would be: Don't chase after every technological trend, because activism only distracts you from the really important tasks.

A few comments on personality

Before we reach the end of this book, I would like to add a few comments on personality and the personal behaviour of executives. These thoughts are based strictly on my own observations, beliefs, and experiences. As such, they are purely empirical in nature, subjective and in no way scientifically proven. However, I am firmly convinced that success in the age of networks is closely tied to leadership and personal attitudes towards our employees, colleagues, and fellow human beings. Readers who do not believe in the value of subjective opinions can simply skip this chapter.

Much of this book is about how important and strategic the role of a CIO is, and about how essential IT is in a world of converging technologies and dematerialisation. This argument should not be interpreted, however, as a call to CIOs and other executives to work hard on their own careers or their personal brand. Quite the opposite. I would instead recommend putting one's ego aside.

Personally, I don't believe in detailed career planning or the setting of precise professional goals. In fact, I have often seen people with ambition make wrong decisions because they were too focused on their own career goals. With your own career planning in mind, you inevitably tend to make all decisions – mostly unconsciously – in a way that you believe will bring you closer to your personal goals. In my experience, these decisions may give you an individual advantage over the short term, but they usually prove to be the wrong decisions over the longer term. This is because we are all part of a larger collective, a company, a community, etc. And what may be good for the individual in the short term is usually bad for the collective overall. I firmly believe that you are more successful in the long term, and do better, if you always make decisions in the interests of the collective.

The second reason for my scepticism about career planning is that having a plan can prevent you from spotting opportunities that appear outside of your own plan, and you will therefore miss them. By contrast, not having a detailed plan can allow you to be more open to opportunities and act quickly at the right moment – a kind of agile model rather than a rigid project plan using the waterfall method. This "agile career planning", if you will, has served me well throughout my professional life.

When I look back over my own career path and imagine that I might have planned it, I wonder: How likely is it that my plan would have worked out in exactly this way? The probability would be close to zero. There have been so many coincidences and fortunate constellations that I could never have planned for or predicted. Of course, I have always worked hard, applied myself, and gone the extra mile to make the greatest possible contribution, but I have also been in the right place at the right time and made decisions instinctively, from the gut: and above all, I was lucky.

My advice? Do not plan too much, be open to challenging opportunities that will yield personal growth, work hard, always try to make the right decisions for the collective, make a positive contribution, and avoid being an arrogant, self-absorbed, or condescending asshole. Do not devote too much time and attention to cultivating your own reputation but set your ego aside and let your work speak for itself. For more, see Rainer Janßen's book, *"Arschlöcher gibt's halt leider überall"*[30].

Unfortunately, it is primarily the "bad guys", the ambitious egomaniacs, who make it into the history books, not those who devote their lives to doing something positive. Important exceptions exist of course, like Mahatma Gandhi or Mother Teresa, people who are still admired

---

30   Janßen, Rainer: *Arschlöcher gibt's halt leider überall.* Epubli Verlag, 2023.

for their self-sacrifice. However, the "good guys" mainly appear in religious books, while history books are sadly full of tyrants like Hitler, Stalin, Mao, Napoleon, and Alexander the Great, those who ruthlessly pursued their personal aims at a cost of thousands or even millions of human lives.

If you work too hard on your own image and your brand, you may have the opportunity to make a name for yourself, but history suggests that you are most likely to achieve this through egotism, narcissism, unfair practices, and the oppression of others. One should not underestimate history; it is one of our best teachers. A famous bit of wisdom often attributed to Winston Churchill is: *"Those who fail to learn from history are doomed to repeat it"*. He also reportedly recommended to a group of prospective students at Oxford University: *"Study history, study history. In history lies all the secrets of statecraft"*[31].

Let's stay on the topic of decision making for a moment. I am an engineer by education and am used to relying on facts and figures when making decisions. Over the course of my professional life, however, I have learnt that not everything relevant can be represented by data. Facts and figures are always a massive oversimplification of reality, and while they can help us to make sense of complex situations, they do not themselves represent reality. In my opinion, it is a major misconception that the massive amounts of data generated by today's networked world will necessarily enable us to make better, fact-based decisions, or that we should rely more on analytical methods. I believe quite the opposite to be true. The deluge of data is tantamount to sensory overload and humans can reasonably process only a certain number of data points in an analytical decision-making process.

---

31   https://winstonchurchill.org/resources/speeches/speeches-about-winston-churchill/the-study-of-history-and-the-practice-of-politics/

For human beings, the challenge is not information quantity but selectivity – not obtaining more data but determining which data matters most. However, if the amount of data is so large that we humans can no longer process it, but algorithms can – well, then two options are open to us:

1. We leave it to AI to analyse the data for us and then let it suggest a decision, i.e., we delegate decision-making to a machine that can handle the large quantities of data better than we humans can.

2. We rely once again on one of humanity's greatest strengths: our instinct, our gut feeling.

I know it may sound a bit strange for me, an engineer and a person immersed in the modern, networked world where almost everything can be measured, to suggest that we should rely more on our gut feeling. I am convinced, however, that humans have a unique and immensely valuable ability to subconsciously form an opinion from millions of impressions, experiences, and data points. How often do the facts say one thing, while your gut feeling says something else?

We are all familiar with the various cost-benefit analysis techniques that people often use to decide on various options. Typically, such an evaluation process begins by drawing up an evaluation grid with a set of criteria, which are then weighted according to their importance. After carefully analysing the available options, we assign a value to each criterion (e.g., a score from 1 to 5). These values are then multiplied by their respective weights, and the totals are compared. This process yields an apparently objective, analytically calculated evaluation for each option. But let's be honest. How often in such situations have you looked at these evaluations and thought to yourself: "That can't be right" because you were expecting a different result and because your gut feeling suggests that the evaluation must be flawed in some way? So, what do you do then? Perhaps you start to adjust the individual values and weights until the results align with what your gut feeling has been telling you all along. At one time or another, many of us have probably been tempted to modify the analytical process until the result produces the same conclusion that our gut feeling (our intuition) had reached at the start.

Why do we do this? Why can we not admit to ourselves from the outset that we often make better decisions based on our gut feeling than we do when we rely purely on analytical methods? In many cases, we arrange the facts to confirm or shore up our intuitive impression. Over the years, I have learned to rely more on my gut feeling when making decisions. Too often in my professional life, I have been seduced by apparent facts, gone against my gut feeling, and regretted it. This is particularly the case with personnel matters, which often involve "soft" factors that are hard to parse analytically. While quantifiable facts and analytical methods are obviously valuable, we should not trust in them blindly. I do not believe in the myth that everything can be measured. The facts are always merely a massive simplification of reality and never the whole reality; the facts lack context and certainly do not include experiences from the past. Of course, I use analytical methods and facts to make decisions, but when in doubt, I go with my gut feeling.

However, gut feelings can also be misleading. We must resist the temptation to jump to conclusions without having looked at the facts and given our subconscious the time to form an opinion from all of our impressions and experiences. Daniel Kahneman describes this situation very well in his book *"Thinking, Fast and Slow"*[32]. He discusses two systems that we use to make decisions: intuition, the fast but error-prone "System 1", and analysis, the slower but more reliable "System 2". In his book, Kahneman explains that the best decision-making strategy

---

32 Kahnemann, Daniel: *Thinking, Fast and Slow.* Farrar, Straus And Giroux, 2011.

SYSTEM 1
Intuition & Instict

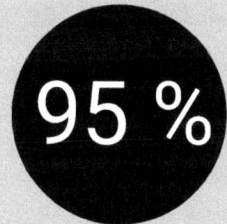

95 %

Unconscious
Fast
Associative
Automatic pilot

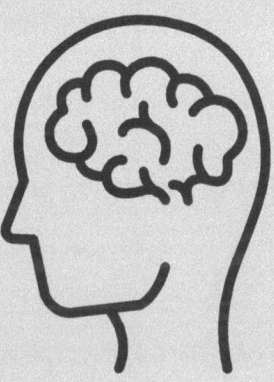

SYSTEM 2
Rational Thinking

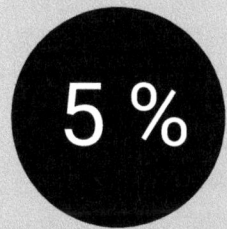

5 %

Takes effort
Slow
Logical
Lazy
Indecisive

employs a sensible combination of the two systems rather than relying entirely on one or the other.

My experience has taught me that my decisions tend to be better when I rely heavily on "System 1", namely intuition. Of course, I do not ignore the facts. My decisions take "System 2" into account, but it is not the dominant system. I have come to realise that my decisions have most often had a bad outcome when I focused entirely on facts (System 2) and ignored my intuition (System 1).

A summary by ChatGPT

In keeping with the Zeitgeist, I asked ChatGPT early 2025 to create a summary of chapters 1 to 19. Even if the summary is not exactly what I wanted to express with this book, I still think it is worth sharing:

The Future Role of the CIO: A Profound Transformation

The role of the CIO has changed dramatically in recent years. Once primarily seen as a technical manager and support figure, the CIO is now a key player in the strategic direction of companies. This shift reflects the increasing integration of technology into all aspects of business. Digitalisation and digital transformation are not just trends but essential drivers for the long-term success of a company.

Digitalisation vs. Digital Transformation

The distinction between digitalisation and digital transformation is crucial. Many companies confuse or equate these two terms, often leading to incomplete or ineffective strategies. While digitalisation involves the automation of existing processes, digital transformation goes much further: it changes the business model, market strategy, and often even the entire corporate culture. This transformation requires a deep understanding of technological possibilities and a bold vision that goes beyond merely improving existing processes.

The Four Stages of Digital Transformation

The four stages described in the text show how differently companies react to the digital challenge:

1. **Digital Cosmetics:** Here, technology is applied superficially, often for image reasons. Such approaches are usually not sustainable, as they don't bring about deep changes.
2. **Digital Silos:** This stage is widespread but carries the risk that companies do not fully leverage the potential of digitalisation. There is a lack of a holistic, interconnected strategy.
3. **Digital Business Model:** Companies like Amazon and Uber have shown how powerful digital business models can be. However, caution is needed here too, as purely digital companies are often vulnerable to disruptions.
4. **Digital Hybrids:** This stage is particularly promising, as it combines the strengths of traditional business models with the advantages of digitalisation. These hybrid models offer stability and flexibility.

The Expanded Role of the CIO

In my view, the CIO must be more than just a technology leader; they must also be a business visionary. The IT department should not operate in isolation but collaborate closely with all areas of the company to develop innovative solutions that create real value. The CIO must bridge the gap between technology and business, ensuring that technological innovations directly contribute to the company's value creation.

Convergence and Virtualisation

The increasing convergence of product, production, and process IT is a complex but necessary undertaking. Uniting these areas requires not only technical know-how but also organisational agility. Virtualisation is another key field that will shape CIOs in the coming years. The ability to transform physical objects and processes into digital forms will enable new business models and efficiency improvements.

Open Innovation and Digital Leadership

Open innovation is more important than ever. Companies that close themselves off from external ideas and technologies risk falling behind. At the same time, leaders, especially the CIO, must drive digital transformation and act as digital leaders. In a world where technology is deeply embedded in all business processes, no leader can afford to ignore digital competence.

Organization: The Shift to Networked Structures

The chapter on organisation highlights the need to rethink traditional hierarchical structures and instead promote networked structures. In a digitalised world, where speed and agility are crucial, rigid hierarchies often become an obstacle. Companies must become more flexible and foster networks rather than hierarchies. This also means that IT departments should not operate in isolation but must be closely intertwined with other areas of the company. The CIO thus becomes not only the head of IT but also the driver of a new, networked organisational culture.

Technology: Integration as the Key to Success

The chapter on technology discusses the increasing merging of product, production, and process IT. Traditionally, these areas were separate, but in a digitalised environment, they must be closely linked. One example of this is the automotive industry, where vehicles are increasingly becoming software-defined products. This requires the IT department to be responsible not only for back-end systems but also for the technologies directly integrated into products. The CIO must ensure that all technological aspects of the company—ranging from production and products to internal processes—are seamlessly integrated to foster innovation and efficiency.

Data: The New Oil

Data is referred to as the "new oil" in the text, highlighting its immense importance for modern businesses. Companies that can effectively collect, analyse, and utilize data can gain deeper insights into their markets and make more informed decisions. The CIO plays a central role in establishing a data-driven culture within the company. This involves not only implementing appropriate technologies for data collection and analysis but also ensuring data quality and security. Additionally, the CIO must align the company's data strategy with its business strategy to maximise value.

Innovation through Technology and Data

The interplay between technology and data creates the foundation for real innovation. Companies must be able to use new technologies like artificial intelligence, IoT, and blockchain to develop innovative products and services. This is where open innovation comes into play, as companies open up their boundaries and include external partners such as start-ups and research institutions. The CIO should actively promote these innovation processes and ensure that technological and data-driven innovations are seamlessly integrated into business processes.

Strategic Importance of IT

Overall, the text emphasises that IT is no longer just a supporting function but a central component of corporate strategy. The role of the CIO is becoming increasingly strategic, as technology and data increasingly form the core of the company. The success of a company thus depends significantly on how well it manages to merge technology, data, and organisation into a harmonious and effective whole.

Conclusion

The future role of the CIO is of enormous strategic importance. In an increasingly digitalised world, CIOs must bring more than just technological skills; they must also demonstrate business thinking, innovation, and leadership. Companies that correctly fill this role and implement the described strategies are most likely to succeed in the digital future.

A summary by NotebookLM (Gemini by Google)

After I finished translating my book into English, I uploaded the text to Google's NotebookLM and asked for a summary of it. This was the output I received in April 2025:

This book, titled "The Technology Illusion: The disenchanted myth of digital transformation," by Patrick Naef, critiques the common understanding and application of digital transformation. It argues that much of what is labelled as digital transformation is merely digitalization, which the author defines as the use of information technologies to automate established business processes within existing business models. True digital transformation, on the other hand, should be transformational, changing the business model, value creation processes, sales channels, or the actual products and services.

The author proposes a four-stage model of digital transformation:

- Stage 1: Digital cosmetics or "lipstick on a pig": This involves superficial adoption of technology for marketing purposes without real integration into business processes.
- Stage 2: Digital silos: Companies automate existing processes within their traditional business model but within isolated organizational units, missing out on potential global optimization.
- Stage 3: Digital or network business model: Companies build entirely digital business models, often acting as intermediaries without physical infrastructure. Examples include Uber, Airbnb, and Amazon (in its early stages).
- Stage 4: Digital hybrids: This involves a combination of traditional and digital business models. Companies with purely digital

models might add physical elements, while traditional companies supplement their offerings with digital products and services. Examples include John Deere and Hilti.

The Book emphasizes the virtualization of physical objects, where many items are disappearing in their physical form and exist as data or services in the cloud or as apps. This trend has significant implications for businesses, requiring them to think beyond physical objects when redesigning processes.

The second part of "The Technology Illusion" delves into various crucial aspects of digital transformation beyond the initial definition and four-stage model.

One significant theme is the strategic role of IT and the CIO. Traditionally viewed as a support function, IT is now becoming a strategic asset and the core of many businesses, especially those dealing with non-physical products like banks and insurance companies. This shift means IT should be seen as a driver of value creation and revenue generation, not just a cost. The convergence of process IT, production IT, and product IT is also highlighted, necessitating closer interaction between these areas. The author argues that future CIOs need to be business-focused, driving the digital agenda across the company, including product innovation. They must also think in networks and exert influence beyond traditional hierarchical structures.

The book extensively discusses the virtualisation of "things". Many physical objects we used decades ago (cameras, books, tickets, etc.) now exist as data or services in the cloud or as apps. This dematerialisation has a fundamental impact on businesses, requiring them to think beyond physical objects when redesigning processes. The marginal cost of virtual objects tends towards zero, and their reproduction and distribution are instantaneous. The author hypothesizes that any object capturing, storing, processing, or displaying information has the potential to be virtualised. This trend also enables interconnectedness between virtual objects, creating new opportunities for innovation. Companies need to consider this virtualisation when automating processes, rather than just automating processes still focused on physical objects.

The book champions open and technology-driven innovation. Relying solely on internal resources for innovation may not be fast enough in the digital age. Tapping into external innovation ecosystems (start-ups, open-source, universities, etc.) can be more efficient. Open innovation requires companies to open up their products and services through APIs and by encouraging contributions from the open-source community. The examples of Google and Apple's app ecosystems illustrate the power of this approach. Corporate venture funds investing in external start-ups are also a way to drive innovation.

The author questions the need for a Chief Digital Officer (CDO), arguing that every leader must become a digital leader. Appointing a CDO can sometimes lead to the creation of silos and internal competition. Instead, the responsibility for digitalisation should be distributed to business leaders, with the CIO acting as a coach and catalyst. Creating numerous "Chief X Officer" roles for every new technology trend is deemed unnecessary and potentially a sign of existing leaders not fulfilling their responsibilities. A business-oriented CIO should drive the digital agenda, making a separate CDO role redundant.

The concept of Shadow IT is also addressed, suggesting that CIOs should see it as a potential benefit rather than a threat. Shadow IT teams are often closer to the business and more agile. The future likely involves a networked structure of IT professionals across the company, rather than a large, centralised IT organisation. The CIO's role should evolve from centralised control to that of a coach and networker.

The book emphasizes the importance of agile methodologies for increasing transparency and speed in software development and beyond. Agile focuses on short iterative cycles (sprints), reducing overhead, and delivering usable code quickly. The goal is to avoid handovers between teams, which slow down processes and can introduce errors. Agile principles can be applied to all areas of a company, and CIOs are well-positioned to drive this transformation. The concept is about maximising the work not done and reducing unnecessary bureaucracy. The trend is also moving towards "bring your own anything (BYOx)", requiring CIOs to manage a diverse range of user-managed devices while ensuring security.

The text discusses the reversal of the outsourcing craze. While outsourcing was once seen as a way to save costs on a non-strategic commodity (IT), many companies now realise that technology is a strategic component and have outsourced too much expertise. Consequently, there's a move towards in-sourcing key IT competencies. However, the ease of consuming cloud services is also acknowledged. The "make or buy" decision for software, especially as it becomes a core part of products and services, is back on the table, with a tendency to bring strategically differentiating software development in-house.

Technology is becoming a critical topic for the board of directors. Despite its strategic importance, few companies have board members with in-depth IT and digital transformation experience. Boards with digital savvy members help companies outperform the competition. Companies need board members who understand how digitalisation can change business models and how to structure the company for the digital age.

The book advocates for networks instead of hierarchies as the dominant organisational model for the digital age. The industrial age model of separating "thinking" and "doing" is no longer optimal. The younger generation's experience with sharing and collaboration highlights the power of networks. Digital transformation breaks down traditional hierarchical silos. The focus should shift from hierarchical structures and reporting lines to the added value and impact individuals can bring. While hierarchies may not disappear entirely, a combination of hierarchies and networks, termed the "quantum organisation", is proposed. This model, drawing an analogy from wave-particle duality in physics, suggests that hierarchies and networks can coexist, with one becoming more dominant depending on the context.

Regarding data, the author emphasizes timeliness and the importance of focusing on changes and trends rather than just absolute figures. The value of data in an operational environment decreases exponentially over time. The common analogy of "data is the new oil" is critiqued, highlighting key differences: data is not scarce, it loses value over time if unused, its value increases with use and sharing, and sharing doesn't diminish the original amount. Leaders should consider these differences when developing data strategies.

In the realm of technologies, the book discusses artificial intelligence (AI) and blockchain. While AI is seen as a significant and promising technology with the potential to achieve "superhuman" abilities for specific tasks, the current hype around generative AI may level off. Blockchain is viewed as having underestimated potential, particularly in simplifying inter-company transactions. A modern CIO must stay informed about the latest technologies but needs to assess their real added value for the company, avoiding chasing every trend.

Finally, the author includes personal observations on personality and leadership. He advises leaders to put their ego aside and focus on the interests of the collective rather than solely on career planning. He also touches upon the importance of instinct and intuition alongside data-driven decisions. The best decisions often involve a combination of intuition and analysis.

A concluding note on the author's book mentions a planned second book featuring guest chapters from experienced individuals, which will further explore the topics discussed.

A note on the author's forthcoming book

Before writing this book, I spoke to various interesting and experienced people about the topics that it would cover. Many of these discussions were so interesting that I asked the people involved if they would be willing to write guest chapters in my book. I was delighted when everyone I asked to write a guest chapter for my book immediately agreed.

However, I swiftly concluded that these guest chapters were so worthwhile in themselves that they deserved a book of their own and should be published as a separate author's book.

I would therefore like to draw your attention to this second, forthcoming book, which will include contributions from various well-known personalities who can further contextualise and elaborate on many of the issues and ideas discussed in this book.

Litterature index

- Bøtter, Jacob/Kolind, Lars: *Unboss*. Jyllands-Postens Forlag, 2012.
- Hamel, Gary/Zanini, Michele: *Humanocracy: Creating Organizations as Amazing as the People Inside Them*. Harvard Business Review Press, 2020.
- Janßen, Rainer: *Arschlöcher gibt's halt leider überall*. Epubli Verlag, 2023.
- Kahnemann, Daniel: *Thinking, Fast and Slow*. Farrar, Straus And Giroux, 2011.
- Kim, Gene/Behr, Kevin/Spafford, George: *The Phoenix Project*. IT Revolution Press, 2018.
- Kiyosaki, Robert: *Rich Dad Poor Dad: What the Rich Teach Their Kids About Money That the Poor and Middle Class Do Not!* Plata Publishing, 2017.
- Rosling, Hans et al.: *Factfulness: Ten reasons we're wrong about the world – and why things are better than you think*. Sceptre, 2018.
- Schwartz, Marc: *The Delicate Art of Bureaucracy: Digital Transformation with the Monkey, the Razor, and the Sumo Wrestler*. IT Revolution Press, 2020.
- Wang, Ray: *Everybody Wants to Rule the World: Surviving and Thriving in a World of Digital Giants*. HarperCollins Leadership, 2021.

Graphics, illustrations and images

- The 4-stage model of digital transformation
    - Lipstick on a pig: © Adobe Stock, generated with AI
    - Digital Silos: © Adobe Stock, generated with AI
    - Digital or network business model: © Tom Goodwin
    - Digital hybrids: Unknown

- The strategic role of IT
    - The future role of IT and the CIO: Illustration: © Patrick Naef

- From a support function to the core of the company
  - Erster motorisierter Flug: © Adobe Stock, by domi002, generated with AI

- The virtualisation of "things"
  - virtualisation of "things": Illustrations: © Patrick Naef
  - New Business Models: Illustration: © Patrick Naef

- Open innovation
  - Open, Connected, Shared & Crowd Sourcing: Illustration: © Patrick Naef
  - Photos: © Patrick Naef

- Every leader must be a digital leader, or: "Who needs a CDO?"
  - «Effective Leader»: Illustration: © David Geurin

- Shorter time-to-market cycles: Everything is becoming agile
  - «Agile Manifesto»: © Sketching Master, Talia McCune, @SketchingSM, https://sketchingmaster.com
  - «Finally we're agile»: © GeekandPoke, 2024, geek-and-poke.com

- Networks instead of hierarchies
  - «Organizational Response to Change: Hierarchical Organizations»: The Behavioral Designers, Illustration: Nina Seitz, © Wikimedia Commons

- A few comments on personality
  - «Traditional CEO vs. Agile CEO»: © Ute Hamelmann, www.utehamelmann.com
  - «Intuition & Instinct vs. Rational Thinking»: Illustration: Nina. Seitz, © Daniel Kahneman